The Readiness GAP

What School and District Leaders Must Know Before Launching MTSS

Dr. Carpia Naylor

Elevate EDSolutions, LLC

Leadership. Systems. Impact.

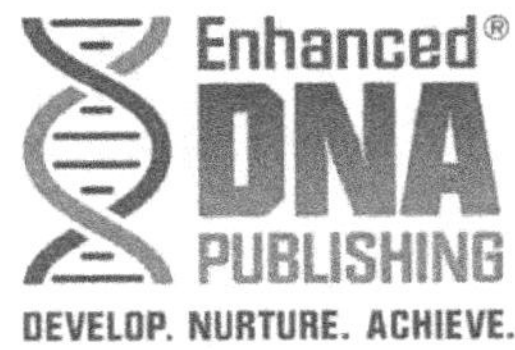

Denola M. Burton
info@EnhancedDNA1.com
www.EnhancedDNAPublishing.com

317-250-5611

THE READINESS GAP
What School and District Leaders Must Know
Before Launching MTSS

ISBN: 978-1-967577-13-2

This book is intended for informational and educational purposes only. The ideas and strategies shared are based on the author's professional experience and are not a substitute for district policy, legal guidance, or individualized decision-making. Readers are encouraged to use their professional judgment when applying the concepts presented.

Preface

This book was written because too many schools are doing *all the right things* and still are not getting the results they were promised when implementing initiatives.

Although this book focuses on Multi-Tiered Systems of Support (MTSS) implementation, the pattern it examines extends far beyond a single framework. Schools today operate within a constant stream of initiatives –literacy reforms, curriculum adoptions, intervention models, coaching systems, and accountability mandates. Each is introduced with urgency and hope. Yet across many systems, the same experience emerges: despite hard work and good intentions, implementation struggles to produce the stability or outcomes leaders expected.

MTSS is widely adopted, mandated, and promoted as the solution to persistent academic, behavioral, and equity challenges. Yet in many systems, outcomes remain inconsistent, staff are overwhelmed, and MTSS becomes another initiative layered on top of an already fragile structure.

I have worked in education long enough to know that the problem is rarely a lack of effort. Educators are working harder than ever. Leaders are navigating competing priorities, policy pressures, and limited resources. The issue is not commitment.

It is readiness.

Over the course of my career, I have held roles spanning classroom instruction, academic coaching, school leadership, district-level systems leadership, and higher education. I have supported schools that were just beginning their MTSS journey and others that believed they were already implementing with fidelity. In both cases, I observed the same pattern: when systems moved to implementation before they were ready, confusion increased. Buy-in eroded. Practices fragmented. And eventually the framework itself was blamed.

This book is grounded in a different premise: MTSS does not fail because educators are incapable or because the framework is flawed. It fails when systems are asked to perform before the conditions for success are in place. This gap reflects what I refer to as "readiness" or more precisely, the absence of it.

Readiness is not a preliminary step to rush through or check off. **It is the work**. It is the leadership's responsibility (district and school) that determines whether MTSS becomes a stabilizing system or another source of strain. Readiness requires leaders to slow down, examine adult practices, align systems, and confront uncomfortable truths about culture, capacity, and equity. That work is often avoided. Not because leaders don't care, but because it demands time, honesty, and sustained attention in environments that oftentimes reward urgency over intention.

This book was written for leaders who are willing to do that work.

It is not a how-to manual for running meetings or selecting interventions. It is not a compliance guide. And it is not a promise of quick fixes. Instead, it is a framework for thinking differently about MTSS and the systems responsible for sustaining it. One that centers leadership, systems, and readiness as the foundation for sustainable implementation.

You will find practical tools in these pages, but more importantly, you will find questions. Questions that help you assess whether your system is prepared to implement MTSS with integrity. Questions that surface gaps before they become failures. Questions that ask not only *what* you are building, but *whether your system is ready to sustain it.*

If you are looking for permission to rush ahead, this book is not for you. But if you are willing to pause, reflect, and lead with intention, especially when doing so feels countercultural, this book will meet you there.

MTSS, when approached with readiness, has the power to transform schools. Not because it adds something new, but because it strengthens what already exists. This book is an invitation to build that foundation deliberately, so that when you do move forward, you are not simply implementing a framework. You are leading a system that is ready to hold it.

Introduction

Schools today are under increasing pressure to meet the diverse needs of students all while responding to new policies, mandates, and accountability expectations. As schools navigate increasing demands to meet the diverse needs of students and respond to state legislative mandates, many struggle to find an effective system that delivers results. Multi-Tiered Systems of Support (MTSS) offers a solution. But for many educators and leaders, the road to implementation is often unclear, challenging, and overwhelming. If that sounds like you, you've picked the right book!

This book examines why MTSS implementation, and many other initiatives, often struggle and what leaders must understand about readiness before systems can succeed. Based on years of experience and proven strategies, this book is designed to empower you to implement MTSS with clarity, purpose, and confidence. Whether you're just getting started or refining an existing system, the insights and tools in this book will help you overcome barriers, build a strong foundation, and achieve sustainable success.

The truth is, MTSS isn't just a framework; it's a commitment to equity, data-driven decision-making, and proactive support for every student. It requires readiness, intentionality, and collaboration at every level. And when done right, MTSS transforms schools, improves outcomes, and ensures that every student receives the right support at the right time.

Through the chapters ahead, you'll learn how to assess your school or district's readiness. In many schools, implementation begins with the visible structures like schedules, intervention blocks, data meetings, and progress monitoring tools. These elements are important, but they are only the surface of a much deeper system. When the underlying conditions for success –shared expectations, aligned leadership, clear routines, and collective responsibility– have not been established, even well-designed frameworks struggle to produce consistent results. Understanding readiness is not simply about improving implementation; it is about strengthening a system's capacity to carry out complex change.

This is the ultimate starting point before any framework or initiative can become successful, and this is also a crucial step that many schools and school districts often miss. Along with readiness comes building the right team, developing essential components, and creating a plan of action that's realistic and doable; one that makes sense for *your* school or district. In this book, you'll also explore the stages of implementation and learn solutions to common implementation challenges. Above all, you'll gain the knowledge and confidence to make MTSS not just another thing to do, but the foundation of how you do school.

So… are you ready to unleash the power of readiness and transform your MTSS system? Let's get started.

How to Use This Book

So here we are–You're holding (or scrolling through) this book because something inside of you knows your school or district needs something different because something in your system is not working the way it should. Everything looks like it's working– meetings are happening, data is analyzed, interventions are scheduled– but outcomes are not reflecting the effort. You've been doing the work, and still, something is off.

This book was written for that moment.

The Readiness Gap is not a checklist or a compliance resource. It is a framework for thinking differently about what must happen before any initiative can succeed. It is a book about sequence, about systems, and about the leadership decisions that determine whether the work you are building will hold or unravel. This book isn't just about Multi-Tiered Systems of Support (MTSS). It's about building the kind of foundation that actually *works* for kids, for staff, and for you as a leader.

Before you dive in, here is what you need to know about how this book is organized and how to get the most out of it.

Why This Book Is Sequenced the Way It Is

The structure of this book is intentional, and the sequence matters.

That is not a random statement. It is the central argument of everything you are about to read. Systems fail when the sequence is wrong. Leaders implement before they are ready. They build structures before the culture can carry them. They launch initiatives before the conditions for success exist. And then they wonder why the work does not hold.

Every chapter was placed where it is for a reason. The earlier chapters establish the conditions under which everything that follows must be understood. Each chapter builds on the one before it, the same way a system must build its readiness before it can sustain implementation.

Here is the logic of the sequence.

The book opens by reframing what MTSS actually is –not a program, not a triangle, not a checklist, but a system that requires specific conditions to function. That reframing is necessary before anything else can land the way it should.

From there, the book moves immediately into equity as a readiness condition. In many MTSS books and professional learning spaces, equity appears near the end, as an add-on, framed as an important consideration to keep in mind. That framing is a problem. Equity is not a consideration. It is a condition. If your system has not examined who is being served, who is being missed, and what existing practices are quietly reproducing disparities, your readiness work has not begun. Equity does not come after planning. It shapes it. That is why it appears here, early, before the culture work, before the process steps, before the tools. Because everything that follows must be built on that foundation.

Once that foundation is established, the book examines culture and adult behavior change as readiness conditions. Not as climate work that happens alongside implementation, but as the ground that determines whether implementation will take hold at all. Systems do not change unless the people within them change first. That reality must be confronted before any process or framework is introduced.

From culture, the book moves into the 5-step planning process –the practical sequence for building readiness before implementation begins. And immediately following that process, the book provides the tools that make the work real. Tools as the instruments you need in hand while you are doing the planning work, not after.

Then, the book turns to the stages of implementation because implementation cannot be understood apart from the readiness that precedes it. By the time you reach that chapter, you will have the context, the conditions, and the instruments to understand what those stages are actually asking of your system.

The book closes its core content with common pitfalls, and they are positioned there intentionally, after the stages, so that you can map each pitfall onto the stage where it most commonly appears.

How to Read This Book

You don't need to read this from start to finish in one sitting. In fact, I don't recommend it. MTSS isn't a sprint, and this book isn't either. You can jump around, reread chapters, dog-ear pages, and bring pieces of it into your team meetings or PD sessions. This book is yours to use however you need.

Here are a few ways leaders have found this book most useful.

Read it to learn, not just to finish. Take notes. Highlight what hits. Let it challenge you. Let the questions in each chapter surface what is working, what is inconsistent, and what your system is not yet ready to carry. The value of this book is not in confirming what you already know. It is in making visible what has been operating beneath the surface.

Use it as a planning guide with your team. Work through the chapters together. Talk about what's working in your school and what isn't. Build your system from a place of shared understanding. Use the tools as shared instruments, not individual exercises. Readiness is not built by one leader reading a book. It is built by a system doing the work collectively.

Return to it when the work gets hard. And it will get hard. There will be moments when urgency overrides intention, when pressure to move forward outweighs the discipline to pause, when the system is moving but not yet stable. Come back to this book in those moments. Not to start over, but to recalibrate.

Use it to spark courageous conversations and meaningful planning. The dilemmas in Appendix A were written for exactly that purpose. And since this book was written with principals, district leaders, MTSS coaches, all educators and changemakers in mind, the dilemmas reflect real decisions leaders face when implementing initiatives inside complex, under-resourced, high-pressure systems. Feel free to use them in leadership retreats, team meetings, and coaching conversations. They are designed to surface tension, challenge assumptions, and sharpen thinking that frameworks alone cannot build.

A Word About the Questions

Throughout this book, you will encounter questions. Some are embedded in the narrative. Some appear at the end of sections as readiness reflections. Some surface in the dilemmas and the FAQs.

The questions in this book are not rhetorical. They are diagnostic. They are designed to reveal the difference between the appearance of readiness and the reality of it. This is at the heart of everything this book is trying to help you see.

If a question stops you, that is the work. If a question makes you uncomfortable, that is the work. If a question reveals something about your system that you have not been naming directly, that is exactly the work this book was written to support.

One Final Thought Before You Begin

Readiness is not something you feel. It is something you build. It is visible in how adults operate, not just in what they say. It is revealed in whether expectations are shared, whether practices are consistent, and whether the system can sustain the work beyond the initial launch.

This book will help you see your system clearly. Not as you hope it is. Not as it appears on paper. But as it actually operates, and how it could operate when the conditions for success are deliberately and intentionally built.

That is the readiness work.

And it starts here.

Table of Contents

Preface iii

Introduction vii

How to Use This Book ix

Chapter 1: Reframing MTSS Through the Lens of Readiness 1

Chapter 2: Equity as a Readiness Condition 15

Chapter 3: Building the Culture and the System for MTSS 23

Chapter 4: The 5-Step Process for Building Readiness 37

Chapter 5: Tools That Tell You the Truth About Readiness 65

Chapter 6: The Stages of Implementation for MTSS 79

Chapter 7: Common Readiness Pitfalls and How to Avoid Them 93

Conclusion: Lead with Readiness. Transform with Purpose 101

Appendix A: Readiness in Practice — Dilemmas for Leaders 105

Appendix B: Frequently Asked Readiness Questions 113

References 119

List of Figures

Figure 1: The Readiness Gap Framework 11

Figure 2: The MTSS Readiness Tool Sequence 75

CHAPTER 1

Reframing MTSS Through the Lens of Readiness

Let me begin by saying that while this book mainly focuses on MTSS, the readiness principles explored here can apply to far more than just the MTSS framework. They can apply to any initiative that schools or districts undertake.

For starters, let's think about all the new initiatives that schools launch each school year. Schools launch these new initiatives with the hope that the implementation of these initiatives will improve outcomes for students, right? But when the underlying conditions for implementation are not established first, even the most promising ideas struggle to take hold. Research on implementation science has repeatedly demonstrated that initiatives are unlikely to succeed when organizations attempt to implement complex change before establishing the necessary supports and conditions for success (Fixsen et al., 2005, 2019; Durlak & DuPre, 2008). MTSS simply provides one of the clearest illustrations of this broader leadership challenge.

MTSS is not a program or a checklist. It is a system intentionally designed to ensure that every student receives the right level of support at the right time, based on data and responsive instruction. When MTSS functions as intended, it aligns academic, behavioral, and social-emotional supports into one coherent framework rather than a collection of disconnected efforts (Sugai & Horner, 2020; McIntosh & Goodman, 2016).

MTSS is often misunderstood because it is introduced as a set of components instead of a way of operating. Schools are trained on tiers, interventions, meetings, and data, but far less attention is given to whether the system itself is ready to support those elements. As a result, MTSS becomes something schools "do" rather than something they are. That distinction matters.

At its core, MTSS is about how schools make decisions. It requires clarity around expectations, consistency in practice, and collective responsibility for student outcomes. When those conditions are absent, MTSS is not unsuccessful; it is premature. When schools or districts implement MTSS, or any initiative, without readiness, it creates the appearance of progress while masking deeper systemic gaps.

One of the most common missteps in MTSS implementation is treating it as a technical solution to complex problems. Leaders search for the right program, the right schedule, or the right intervention, believing that implementation alone will produce results. And when it doesn't flow the way they think it should, they say, "MTSS doesn't work". MTSS does not fail because the framework is flawed. It fails because it's launched before the conditions for success are set in place. That, my friend, means the system was not ready.

The challenge with MTSS is not understanding its components. It is committing to the work that must happen ***before*** those components can function. MTSS exposes whether systems are aligned, whether adult practices are consistent, and whether leadership has established the conditions necessary for sustained implementation. That level of exposure can be uncomfortable, which is why readiness work is often rushed or avoided.

This is why MTSS is, first and foremost, a leadership responsibility. Leaders determine whether a system is ready to launch, ready to scale, or not ready at all. When readiness is overlooked, MTSS becomes another initiative that strains staff and delivers inconsistent outcomes. When readiness is prioritized, MTSS becomes a stabilizing force rather than an additional burden.

Understanding MTSS is not about memorizing terminology or adopting new tools. It is about recognizing that student outcomes are a reflection of adult systems, and those systems must be prepared before they are expected to perform.

What Do I Mean by Readiness?

Let me step back. When I talk about readiness, I am not referring to enthusiasm, motivation, or the completion of preliminary tasks. I'm talking about being prepared. Sometimes, readiness is confused with momentum. Teams attend training sessions on an initiative, schedules and routines are adjusted, and data is introduced and analyzed. From the outside, it looks like progress. But just because activity is happening doesn't mean the system is ready. A system can be "busy" and still be unprepared.

Readiness has been referred to as the extent to which an organization is both *willing* and *able* to implement a particular practice (Dymnicki et al., 2014). Organizational readiness reflects the collective capacity of leaders and staff to successfully implement and sustain new practices (Weiner, 2009). Readiness is the system's ability to operate with clarity, consistency, and collective responsibility before the work begins. It includes leadership alignment, staff capacity, coherent data systems, shared expectations, and the structures that support follow-through. Readiness answers one essential question:

Is this system prepared to perform the work it is being asked to do?

Readiness is not a feeling. It is a system. Many times, I have seen leaders rely on instinct when determining whether they are ready to move forward or not with implementing a new initiative or framework. They look for signs like buy-in, excitement, or urgency, and while those elements can be helpful, they are not indicators of readiness. Again, readiness is not something you feel. It is a system you build. It is created through intentional alignment. It is visible in how adults operate, not just in what they say. It is reflected in whether expectations are shared, whether practices are consistent, and whether the system can sustain the work beyond initial implementation.

The Core Components of Readiness

In order to understand readiness more precisely, we must first examine it in terms of how it shows up across the entire system. Readiness may look different depending on the context, but high-functioning systems consistently demonstrate alignment across several critical areas. Let's discuss those.

First and foremost, readiness begins with leadership alignment.

Leadership alignment is not simply a matter of agreement in meetings. Alignment is in consistency in decisions, in messaging, and in expectations across every level of the system. In systems where leadership is aligned, priorities remain stable, direction is clear, and staff experience coherence rather than confusion. When leadership alignment is absent, messaging can shift depending on who is speaking, initiatives compete for attention, and staff are left to interpret expectations on their own. In those circumstances, even the best of frameworks will struggle to take hold because the system lacks stability.

Closely connected to leadership alignment is capacity. Mainly adult capacity.

Building capacity is often misunderstood as professional development, but readiness demands far more than mere exposure to the initiative in a professional learning setting. It requires that the people responsible for the work possess the knowledge, skills, and confidence they need to carry the new initiative out consistently. In systems where capacity has been intentionally developed, professional learning is ongoing and embedded into daily practice. Staff are not only trained; they are supported through coaching, feedback, and opportunities to refine their work. When capacity is underdeveloped, implementation is spotty. Educators are asked to execute practices they do not fully understand, and variability in how the initiative is executed becomes the norm.

Beyond leadership and capacity, readiness depends on coherence.

Coherence is what allows a system to function as a system rather than a collection of disconnected, siloed efforts. In MTSS implementation especially, it reflects alignment between instruction and intervention, between academic, behavioral, and social-emotional supports, and between data systems and decision-making processes. In schools and districts where there are coherent systems, practices reinforce one another and teams operate within shared expectations. In incoherent systems, teams work in parallel rather than in partnership. Data may be collected, but it is not consistently used to inform instructional decisions. No matter how hard an individual's efforts are, this isolation can limit the system's overall effectiveness.

Readiness is also evident in the structures that support the work.

Structures provide the routines and processes that make consistency possible. We must have clearly defined roles, established protocols for collaboration, and predictable systems for using data and delivering support. In systems where structures are functioning effectively, teams know who is responsible for what, meetings lead to action, and processes are followed consistently. In systems where structures are weak or unclear, roles become blurred, meetings lack direction or follow-through, initiatives exist on paper but not in practice, and implementation depends more on an individual or select individuals rather than on system design.

Finally, readiness requires accountability.

Expectations alone do not create change. They must be upheld and reinforced through consistent follow-through. In systems where accountability is present, expectations are applied across all staff; leaders monitor implementation and provide feedback, and inconsistencies are addressed directly rather than ignored. In systems where accountability is lacking, follow-through is inconsistent, accountability varies depending on the situation or individual, and expectations gradually become optional. Over time, this erodes trust in the system and weakens the integrity of the work.

These elements form the foundation of readiness. When these core components are aligned, systems operate with clarity and purpose. When they are not, implementation becomes strained, regardless of how strong the framework may appear on paper.

What Does Readiness Look Like in Practice?

For one thing, it shows up in the way a school or district operates on a day-to-day basis. There is a sense of clarity. People understand what is expected of them, and more importantly, they understand why it matters. Decisions are not made in isolation. Teams are not working in silos. There is alignment in how people talk about the work, how they approach it, and how they follow through.

You don't see constant starts and stops with initiatives. You don't see one classroom operating completely differently from the one next door. You don't hear five different interpretations of what MTSS is, depending on who you ask. You see consistency. You see shared ownership. You see a system that, while not perfect, is stable enough to hold the work. And, ultimately, you start to see results.

In a system that is ready, meetings are not just meetings. They lead to action. Data is not just reviewed; it is used. Conversations are not surface-level; they push thinking and lead to decisions. When something is not working, it is addressed, not avoided.

There is also a level of predictability. Not rigidity, but predictability. Staff know what will happen, when it will happen, and how decisions will be made. That predictability creates trust. And trust is what allows people to fully engage in the work, even when it is challenging.

But let's be just as clear about the other side.

When readiness is missing, you can see that too.

It looks like constant motion with very little momentum. Teams are meeting, but nothing is changing. Data is being collected, but no one is quite sure what to do with it. Expectations exist, but they are interpreted differently across classrooms, grade levels, or buildings. Leaders are saying the right things, but those messages are not translating into consistent practice.

In these systems, you often hear phrases like, "We tried that," or "That doesn't work here." The work itself is not to blame; the system was never prepared to support it in the first place.

It also shows up in the strain people feel.

Teachers feel like they are being asked to do more without clarity. Coaches feel like they are supporting in pockets instead of across a system. Leaders feel like they are constantly putting out fires instead of leading a coherent strategy. Over time, that strain turns into fatigue. And fatigue turns into disengagement.

So when you're thinking about readiness, don't just think about what is written in your plans or what has been scheduled on your calendar. Look at how your system actually operates. Look at what is consistent, what is unclear, and what is being tolerated.

Readiness is not what you say you're doing.

It's what your system is actually able to sustain.

Why Readiness Is Often Skipped

I'm sure you're asking: if readiness is so important, why do so many schools and districts often skip it?

Here's my answer: it's not that leaders don't understand the value of planning and preparation; it's that the conditions they are working in make it difficult to prioritize.

Schools and districts operate in environments that reward urgency, and planning takes time. There are timelines to meet, mandates to follow, and expectations to show progress quickly. Leaders are asked to implement new initiatives while still maintaining everything else that already exists. In that kind of environment, slowing down to assess readiness can feel like falling behind.

So what happens?

Leaders move forward because they feel like they have to.

They build schedules, launch initiatives, and introduce new practices not because the system is fully prepared, but because the pressure to act outweighs the space to reflect. From the outside, it looks like progress. Internally, it feels like trying to build something while it's already in motion.

There's also a human side to this that we don't talk about enough.

Readiness requires leaders to look at their systems and ask difficult questions about alignment, consistency, and effectiveness. It requires acknowledging where things are not working as well as they should be. And for many leaders, that level of reflection and transparency can feel risky. Not because they are avoiding the work, but because they are navigating systems where vulnerability is not always rewarded or supported.

Another reason readiness is skipped is because it is often misunderstood as something that can happen quickly, like in a few days or weeks. That's not the case.

Readiness is not a phase you rush through. It is the work that determines whether everything that follows will hold. It's not completely separate from implementation, but it is what makes implementation possible.

And here is the part that leaders often learn the hard way:

When readiness is skipped, the system may keep moving for a while, but it does so under a level of strain. And over time, that strain doesn't just weaken the work, it causes it to collapse.

Then implementation becomes harder than it needs to be. Staff require more support, more clarification, and more correction. Leaders spend more time addressing breakdowns than building forward momentum. What could have been established upfront has to be repaired in the middle of the work. And that is far more difficult.

Slowing down at the beginning does not delay progress.

It protects it.

So if you find yourself feeling the pressure to launch MTSS or any other initiative quickly, pause and ask:

Are we moving forward because we are ready?

Or are we moving forward because we feel like we have to?

Readiness Before Implementation

Here is where many systems get it wrong, and it's not because of a lack of effort. It's because of how the work is approached. Unfortunately, many schools and districts that roll out MTSS frameworks jump straight into implementation when they really should begin with readiness work.

When leaders put structures in place, the system appears to be functioning. On the surface, it looks like progress. The pieces are there. The work has started.

But something doesn't quite hold.

It doesn't hold because the sequence is off. Implementation has now become the entry point.

When implementation becomes the entry point, systems are forced to build clarity, alignment, and capacity while simultaneously trying to execute the work.

And that is where the strain begins.

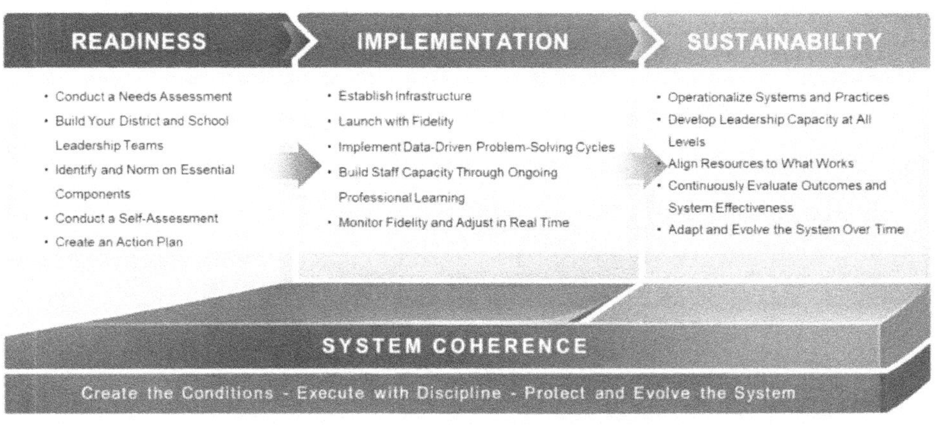

Figure 1.

The Readiness Gap Framework

Here is my signature Readiness Gap Framework to illustrate the proper sequencing and the actions that accompany each sequence.

This framework represents the full MTSS journey, from preparation to sustainability. It makes visible what is often overlooked: that implementation is only the *middle* of the work, not the beginning. Let's walk through each stage.

The first stage is **Readiness.**

Readiness is where clarity is established, expectations are aligned, staff capacity is built, and systems are prepared to function coherently. This is where adult practices are examined, roles are clarified, and the conditions for success are intentionally designed. Without readiness, MTSS becomes procedural rather than systemic. This book will examine this stage in greater detail in the remaining chapters.

The second stage **is Implementation.**

In MTSS, this is where Tier 1 instruction, targeted supports, intensive interventions, and progress monitoring come to life. Implementation is the visible work of MTSS, but it can only function effectively when readiness has already been established. When systems skip readiness, implementation exposes inconsistency rather than strength. At this stage, structures, schedules, roles, and decision-making protocols become operational, not theoretical. Regular, disciplined problem-solving cycles are taking place, not sporadic data conversations. Capacity is being built through job-embedded coaching, modeling, and feedback loops, not one-off PDs. And implementation is being actively managed and monitored, not just passively observed.

The final stage **is Sustainability.**

Sustainability must serve as system protection and continuous refinement. This stage reflects a system's ability to maintain effective practices over time through coaching, fidelity, continuous improvement, and shared accountability. Sustainability is not achieved through effort alone; it is the result of readiness and disciplined implementation working together. At this stage, schools and districts have embedded implementation into policies, schedules, and expectations so the work doesn't just live with one person or department. Leadership is distributed. Resources such as time, staffing, and funding have been aligned to what is working and not individual preferences. System effectiveness and outcomes are continuously evaluated, not just student data. The entire system is evolving over time and adjustments are made that set the system up for continued success.

Beneath all three stages is **System Coherence.**

System coherence represents alignment across all domains. It is what allows MTSS to function as an integrated system rather than fragmented parts. When coherence is weak, even strong initiatives struggle to take hold.

This framework reveals a truth many schools experience but rarely name: MTSS often fails when readiness is missing, not in implementation.

This foundation sets the stage for the work ahead. Before schools can implement MTSS with fidelity, they must assess and build readiness across leadership, instruction, data use, and culture. That work begins with leadership and extends to every corner of the system.

CHAPTER 2

Equity as a Readiness Condition

The chapters of this book focus on the visible work of readiness: planning, structures, teams, tools, and preparation steps that must be in place before MTSS implementation begins. But readiness is not only technical; it is also deeply human. Equity matters at the readiness stage because unexamined biases, inequitable practices, and blind spots in adult decision-making can quietly derail MTSS before it ever gets off the ground. If leaders do not confront how race, language, ability, and access show up in their systems during the planning phase, even the most well-intentioned MTSS efforts will reproduce the very disparities they aim to disrupt. Equity work, done early, clears the path. Without it, MTSS implementation is built on unstable ground, no matter how strong the structures appear to be.

At the core of MTSS is a promise that every student, regardless of background, identity, or circumstance, deserves the opportunity to succeed. But let's be clear: equity doesn't just happen because we say the word in staff meetings or drop it into our mission statements. It requires systems-level readiness, intentional reflection, and brave decisions.

Equity is not the destination; it's the reason we build the road in the first place.

Research on equity-centered school improvement consistently shows that systems designed without intentional attention to equity often reproduce existing disparities rather than eliminate them (Skiba et al., 2016). When schools fail to ask how race, language, and access intersect with instructional systems, interventions can inadvertently reinforce inequitable patterns rather than disrupt them.

Too often, schools approach MTSS and equity as separate initiatives. One is about interventions. The other is about justice. But in reality, they are inseparable. You cannot implement MTSS with fidelity if your system isn't ready to confront inequity head-on. Readiness, in this context, means being prepared to look closely at who is being served, who is being missed, and what the system might be doing intentionally or not, to reinforce disparities.

Research examining MTSS and schoolwide intervention systems supports this connection. Studies have found that MTSS frameworks are most effective when they explicitly incorporate culturally responsive practices and equity-focused data analysis (Sullivan et al., 2022). When equity is not intentionally embedded, tiered systems may unintentionally mirror the same inequities present in the broader educational system.

Here's the truth: readiness for MTSS is incomplete without equity. A district may have teams, tools, and timelines in place, but if it hasn't built the will, the awareness, and the courage to interrogate disparities, it's not ready. So what does equity-readiness look like?

It looks like disaggregated data being used in every decision-making space—not just in one compliance report a year. It looks like teams that ask not just "what's working?" but "who is this working for?" It looks like leaders who are willing to pause implementation not out of fear, but out of respect for doing the work right.

Data transparency is a critical component of equity-centered systems. Research on discipline, intervention access, and academic outcomes consistently shows that disaggregated data reveal patterns of disproportionality that often remain invisible in aggregated reports (Skiba et al., 2016). When schools regularly analyze data by race, language status, disability, and socioeconomic status, they are better positioned to identify inequities and respond proactively.

If your Tier 2 interventions are full of Black boys with behavioral referrals but those same students aren't represented in enrichment, your system isn't ready.

If your English learners are consistently in Tier 3 but the instructional core doesn't include language scaffolds, your system isn't ready.

If your MTSS team is diverse in job titles but homogenous in lived experience, and no one is questioning that, your system isn't ready.

Research has shown that disparities in intervention placement, disciplinary referrals, and access to advanced learning opportunities are often linked to systemic practices rather than individual student deficits (Scott, et al., 2025).

Readiness for equity in MTSS means being willing to ask the hard questions and being ready to uncover the answers:

Are our data practices revealing disparities or concealing them?

Do our policies inadvertently gatekeep access to supports?

Are our interventions designed with cultural responsiveness in mind, or are we asking students to conform to a norm that doesn't reflect them?

Schools that are ready for equity-centered MTSS create systems that don't just react to gaps; they work to prevent them. That means embedding culturally responsive practices into Tier 1, establishing clear and fair criteria for intervention access, and inviting families and communities to the table, not as guests, but as co-designers.

Culturally responsive school leadership research emphasizes that equity-centered systems require shared decision-making and authentic community engagement (Khalifa et al., 2016). Schools that include families and community voices in decision-making are more likely to design systems that reflect the needs and strengths of the students they serve.

This work isn't about perfection. It's about preparation. Equity work in MTSS is ongoing, deeply human, and can be messy. But readiness gives us a framework for doing that work with clarity, instead of chaos.

Where Inequity Shows Up

Believe it or not, inequity is present long before the work officially starts. It shows up in how systems currently operate, often in ways that feel familiar, normalized, or even unnoticeable. Because of that, it is frequently overlooked during readiness work, only to resurface later as inconsistent outcomes or increased demand for intervention.

One of the most common places inequity appears is within Tier 1 instruction.

When instruction varies significantly from one classroom to another, students are not receiving the same level of access to learning. Some classrooms provide strong, standards-aligned instruction with clear expectations and consistent engagement. Others do not. As I've mentioned in this book previously, in these environments, student performance begins to reflect the variability in instruction rather than the actual learning needs of the student.

As a result, intervention systems become overloaded, not because students inherently require more support, but because the core experience is not consistent enough to meet their needs. This is an equity issue within readiness.

Inequity also shows up in how decisions are made about student support. Referral patterns often reflect inconsistencies in expectations rather than differences in student need. Some students are identified for additional support quickly, while others are not identified at all. Behavioral interpretations, teacher perceptions, and levels of tolerance can all influence who receives support and when. When these patterns are not examined, the system begins to respond to perception rather than data. And when that happens, access to support becomes uneven.

Did you know that data itself can also become a source of inequity? In some systems, data is consistently collected but interpreted differently across teams, schools, and teachers. That's why districts and schools need to create a shared understanding of what the data means and how it should guide decisions. Otherwise, teams begin to rely on individual judgment, and over time, this leads to inconsistent responses to similar student needs.

Leadership decisions can further reinforce these patterns.

When expectations are not clearly defined or when follow-through is inconsistent, variability becomes embedded in the system. Schools or classrooms may operate differently under the same framework, and those differences directly impact student experiences and outcomes.

What begins as flexibility becomes inconsistency. And inconsistency becomes inequity.

These patterns are not always intentional. They are often the result of systems operating without the alignment, clarity, and accountability needed to produce consistent outcomes.

Intent does not determine impact. If inequities exist within the system before implementation begins, implementation will not fix that; it will reproduce whatever the system was already producing.

This is why equity is not an initiative. It is a readiness condition that determines whether the system can function as intended.

The Equity Decision Lens

If equity is to function as a condition of readiness, it must shape how decisions are made, right?

This requires more than awareness. It requires a consistent lens that leaders must apply as they design, evaluate, and refine their systems.

Before moving forward with implementation decisions, leaders should be asking:

- **Who is actually benefiting from how your system currently operates?**

  Patterns of success often reveal where the system is working well, so pay attention to who is consistently doing well because that tells you where the system is working. But it also reveals where it is not. If certain groups of students consistently perform better, it is worth examining what conditions are making that possible, and whether those conditions available to all students.

- **Where is variability creating unequal access?**

  Differences in instruction, expectations, or support may be subtle, but their impact is not. Not all variability is harmless. Variability across classrooms, teams, or schools often leads to differences in students' experience and opportunities, and that's not about need. That is about the system.

- **Are we responding to need, or to visibility?**

  Students who struggle in visible ways are often identified more quickly than those whose needs are less apparent. The students who struggle loudly get attention first, and the ones who struggle quietly often get missed. Systems must ensure that identification and support are driven by data, not by who raises their hand, acts out, or draws attention. If your system relies on who gets noticed, it's not functioning as a system.

- **Are our decisions producing consistency across contexts or just activity?**

  A system is only as strong as its ability to deliver consistent experiences. A real system produces consistent experiences, no matter the classroom, team, teacher, or building. If decisions lead to different outcomes depending on where or by whom they are implemented, the system is not yet ready.

- **What needs to be fixed in the system, not added on top of it, to ensure equitable outcomes?**

  The instinct is always to add more –more interventions, more programs, more support. But more is rarely the real issue. The better question is: what is it in the core system that must be improved to reduce the need for more on top of what's already there?

Equity readiness is a mindset and a system. And MTSS gives us the structure, if we're willing to do the work.

If your MTSS implementation plan doesn't address equity explicitly, revise it.

If your data meetings don't include questions about disproportionality, change them. If your Tier 1 instruction isn't culturally sustaining, rebuild it.

Equity won't show up in your system unless you build a system that's ready for it. That's the work. And that's where MTSS begins…not with tiers, but with the truth.

CHAPTER 3

Building the Culture and the System for MTSS

Before schedules are built, interventions selected, or teams convened, schools must be ready to operate as a system. That readiness is not only technical, but also cultural. The beliefs, routines, expectations, and behaviors of adults determine whether MTSS can function as a coherent system or collapse under inconsistency. Culture is not a backdrop for MTSS; it is a readiness condition that determines whether implementation will succeed.

Schools often focus on the visible structures of MTSS: meetings, data protocols, intervention menus, etc. all without attending to whether the culture is prepared to support those structures. When culture is overlooked, MTSS becomes procedural rather than systemic. The pieces may exist, but they do not work together. Readiness is revealed not by what is scheduled, but by how consistently adults operate within their shared expectations. Let me be very clear, MTSS doesn't fail because students don't respond. MTSS fails when we, the adults, don't change.

MTSS requires a shift in how adults respond to student needs. It moves schools from reactive decision-making to intentional, proactive support. That shift cannot occur in a system that is not ready to examine itself. So, in other words, MTSS is about ABC--Adult Behavior Change. Adult behavior change is not a result of MTSS; it is a prerequisite for it. If adults in your system operate with inconsistent expectations, fragmented decision-making, or selective accountability, your system is not ready for MTSS implementation. The question is not whether you have MTSS structures in place. The question is whether your culture can sustain them.

When adults are unwilling or unprepared to align practices, reflect honestly, and follow through consistently, the system is not ready for MTSS.

Adult behavior change is often where I've seen readiness gaps become most visible. Inconsistent routines, uneven expectations, and fragmented decision-making are frequently tolerated because addressing them requires difficult conversations (that some leaders don't want to have) and sustained leadership attention (that leaders don't have time to give). MTSS exposes these inconsistencies quickly. When readiness work has been skipped, implementation reveals strain rather than strength.

Culture is shaped by what leaders reinforce, what they allow to persist, and what they choose *not* to address. When expectations vary widely from classroom to classroom, students experience the system as unpredictable. When data is reviewed but not acted upon, staff learn that meetings are symbolic rather than purposeful. These patterns are not signs of resistance; they are indicators that the system was not fully prepared to function as intended.

Collaboration is often named as a core value of MTSS, yet collaboration without readiness leads to confusion. Effective MTSS teams share responsibility, but they also operate with clear roles, defined decision-making processes (McIntosh & Goodman, 2016), and shared accountability. Collaboration does not mean consensus on every decision; it means collective ownership of outcomes within a system that is prepared to support that work.

Leadership plays a critical role in establishing readiness. When MTSS is delegated without ownership, it becomes disconnected from daily practice. When leaders engage inconsistently, the system loses coherence. Readiness requires visible leadership involvement—not to control the work, but to model alignment, learning, and follow-through. Leaders create the conditions (Fullan, 2007) that determine whether MTSS is going to be sustained or short-lived .

Support and accountability are not implementation strategies; they are readiness conditions. Support ensures educators have the tools, time, and training needed to implement with fidelity (Durlak & DuPre, 2008). Accountability ensures expectations are not optional and inconsistencies are addressed rather than normalized. A system cannot be ready without both. When one is present without the other, MTSS structures struggle to function as designed.

Culture does not shift through messaging alone. It shifts through repeated actions that signal what matters. When professional learning, feedback, data use, and leadership decisions are aligned, readiness is strengthened. When those elements remain misaligned, MTSS becomes an initiative layered onto existing practices rather than a system that reshapes it.

Readiness is visible long before implementation begins. It shows up in how adults collaborate, how consistently expectations are applied, and how willing leaders are to address misalignment. Schools that appear busy but inconsistent are often moving forward without being ready. MTSS implementation may still occur, but it will require far more effort to sustain and far more repair once cracks appear.

Culture and adult behavior change are not parallel to MTSS planning. They are the readiness work that makes planning meaningful. Schools that skip this step often move quickly into design and implementation, only to discover that their systems cannot sustain the work. Readiness is established when leadership has aligned expectations, routines, and accountability across the system. Only then does planning move beyond intention and become a foundation for action.

The triangle is often what we visualize when we have discussions about MTSS, but here's what you really need to know: MTSS isn't just about the triangle or the tiers; it's a way of doing school. It's the foundation that holds everything together, from classroom instruction to school-wide policies. When schools view MTSS as a system, a culture, and a mindset shift, they begin to unlock its full potential. Let's break it down further.

MTSS is a System

MTSS is not just an intervention model, it's an integrated system designed to align and streamline supports across academics, behavior, and social-emotional learning (SEL) (Sugai & Horner, 2020; McIntosh & Goodman, 2016). Thinking of MTSS solely as the triangle is like looking at one piece of a puzzle and ignoring the bigger picture. If MTSS is not seen as a system, it risks being implemented in silos, where academics, behavior, and SEL each operate independently rather than as part of a unified strategy. If your academic and behavioral teams do not share data, share responsibility, or share outcomes, you are not operating as a system. You are operating in parallel, and parallel systems cannot sustain MTSS.

Imagine a school where the academic intervention team and the behavior support team operate separately, each with its own data, its own meetings, and its own action plans. The academic team is tracking struggling students in reading and math, while the behavior team is managing discipline referrals. That's a lot of meetings, a lot of data, and a lot of action plans that could all be streamlined if the system allowed. Now, imagine if the two teams worked together. What if they combined their data to see if struggling students were also experiencing behavioral challenges? What if they collaborated to create support systems that addressed both academic and behavioral needs simultaneously? That's the power of MTSS as a system. Here's why:

MTSS provides:

1. **A unified, strategic approach** to supporting any and all students' needs at all levels, ensuring that interventions are not isolated but part of a larger, integrated framework.
2. **A structured process** for using data to inform instruction, interventions, and decision-making.
3. **A bridge between school initiatives**, preventing fragmented efforts and creating coherence across academic, behavioral, and social-emotional programs.

What System Coherence Actually Requires

Now that we've established that MTSS is a system, not a collection of parts, we have to move beyond the idea and get to the reality of how that system actually works. Here's where many schools and districts believe they are "doing MTSS," but what they are actually doing is managing disconnected efforts and have attached the term MTSS to it.

A system is defined by the alignment of structures.

MTSS only functions as a system when four core domains operate in alignment: instruction, intervention, data, and leadership. When these domains are aligned, the system is coherent. When they are not, the system becomes fragmented. And when fragmentation exists, readiness is not present, whether the system recognizes it or not.

Let's be clear about what this means in practice.

Tier 1 instruction is the foundation of the entire system. It is where MTSS either stabilizes or begins to break down. When Tier 1 instruction is consistent, aligned, and responsive, it reduces the need for intervention and creates a predictable experience for students across classrooms. It provides a stable base where the majority of students can succeed because expectations, instructional practices, and access to learning are aligned.

But when instruction is inconsistent, everything else in the system begins to compensate for that inconsistency. Have you ever observed where one classroom may operate with strong, standards-aligned instruction, and the classroom next door does not? Or, one teacher uses data to adjust instruction daily, while another relies on pacing alone. In these kinds of environments, Tier 1 stops functioning as a foundation and becomes a variable.

And when Tier 1 becomes a variable, it is no longer consistent across the system. Students' learning experiences depend on which classroom they are in rather than on a coherent instructional model. One teacher may be delivering high-quality, standards-aligned, responsive instruction, while another is not. One classroom may have strong engagement and clarity, while another lacks structure or alignment. At that point, Tier 1 is no longer functioning as a dependable baseline.

Once that happens, the system loses its stability, usually for two reasons:

First, student outcomes begin to reflect the variability in instruction rather than students' actual learning gaps. The system can no longer accurately identify who truly needs additional support because the baseline itself is uneven.

Second, intervention demand becomes artificially inflated. Students are referred to Tier 2 or Tier 3 not because they require intensified support, but because they did not receive a consistent Tier 1 experience. Intervention begins to absorb the consequences of weak or inconsistent core instruction, which it was never designed to do.

At that point, the tiers stop functioning as a system of support and start functioning as a system of compensation.

This is what makes the system unstable. The foundation is no longer holding. Everything above it – intervention, data decisions, resource allocation—has to adjust to account for variability at the core. And when the core is unstable, the entire system becomes reactive instead of predictive, fragmented instead of connected.

So the issue is not simply that Tier 1 needs improvement. The issue is that once Tier 1 becomes inconsistent, the system loses its ability to operate as a system at all.

This is where intervention often enters the picture as a response to a problem that was never meant to be solved at the intervention level. Instead of extending instruction, intervention begins to replace it. Students are pulled for support because the core itself is not consistently meeting their needs. Over time, intervention systems become overloaded, not necessarily because students require more support, but because the system has not established a strong enough instructional foundation to reduce that need.

This is not an intervention issue. It is a coherence issue.

Intervention, when aligned, is designed to work in direct connection with instruction. It builds on what happens in the classroom. It reinforces it. It targets specific needs without creating a separate experience for the student. Students should not feel like they are entering a different system when they move into Tier 2 or Tier 3 supports. The expectations, language, and instructional focus should remain connected.

But when intervention is disconnected from Tier 1 instruction, students experience fragmentation. They receive one type of instruction in the classroom and another during intervention. Strategies do not align. Language does not carry over. Progress becomes difficult to measure because the system itself is not operating as one.

At that point, the system is not supporting students more effectively. It is creating multiple, competing versions of support.

This is where the role of data becomes critical, yet it's often misunderstood.

In a coherent system, data is not collected for the sake of compliance. It is used to make decisions that directly impact instruction and intervention. Teams look at the same data sets, interpret it through a shared lens, and respond in ways that are consistent across the system. Data answers questions. It drives action. It creates clarity.

But if the system is fragmented, data just becomes noise.

Different teams use different data sources. Meetings are held, but decisions are unclear. Data is reviewed, but not acted upon. Or worse, decisions are made based on opinion because the system has not established clear expectations for how data should be used. When this happens, the system begins to operate on individual interpretation rather than collective responsibility.

And once data loses its role as the driver of decision-making, the system loses its ability to function predictably.

So now, we have instruction that varies, intervention that compensates, and data that does not consistently guide action. At this point, the system is misaligned. But the question becomes, why does that misalignment persist?

The answer is leadership.

Leadership is what integrates the system. It is what ensures that instruction, intervention, and data are not operating in isolation, but in alignment. Leadership establishes priorities. It reinforces expectations. It determines whether the system operates with consistency or variability.

When leadership is aligned, the system reflects that alignment. Messaging is consistent. Expectations are clear across buildings and classrooms. Decisions reinforce the same priorities over time. Leaders are present in the work, not removed from it. They monitor implementation, address inconsistencies, and ensure that the system is functioning as intended.

But when leadership is misaligned, everything else follows.

Different leaders communicate different expectations. Initiatives compete for attention. One priority is emphasized in one setting, while another takes precedence somewhere else. Staff are left to interpret what matters most, and in the absence of clarity, they default to what is most familiar or most manageable.

At that point, the system is operating as a collection of individual practices held together by a so-called MTSS label.

This is the readiness gap.

This gap does not exist because schools lack effort, resources, or knowledge of MTSS. It is created when these four domains –instruction, intervention, data, and leadership– are not aligned to function together. It is the space between having the components of MTSS and having a system that can actually sustain them.

What some leaders don't realize is that you can have strong instruction in pockets and still have a readiness gap. You can have intervention structures in place and still have a readiness gap. You can collect data consistently and still have a readiness gap. You can even have leaders who are committed to the work and still have a readiness gap.

Because readiness is not just about the presence of each domain. It is about their alignment and how they function together as a system of support.

When these domains operate independently, the system experiences strain. Teachers feel it in the inconsistency of expectations. Teams feel it in meetings that do not lead to action. Leaders feel it in the constant need to address breakdowns rather than build forward momentum. Over time, that strain becomes fatigue. And fatigue becomes disengagement.

And eventually, the system reaches a point where it appears that MTSS is not working.

But MTSS is not the issue. The issue is that pieces of the work needed to prepare a strong system were missing.

This is why alignment is not something that can be assumed. It must be intentionally built. It must be monitored. And it must be protected through leadership decisions that prioritize alignment over activity.

Remember, systems do not fail because pieces are missing. Those missing pieces and gaps can be filled. It's when the pieces are not aligned to begin with that starts to create the failure and breakdown.

MTSS is a Culture, Not a Checklist

Have you ever heard someone say, "*We do MTSS at our school*"? Here's the thing, we don't *"do"* MTSS; we are MTSS. MTSS is not something to check off a list. It's something we become. It's the DNA of a school that's woven into every single interaction, decision, and process in that building. But if your culture is not ready, MTSS will always default to a checklist.

Think about a school where teams only talk about MTSS occasionally during scheduled meetings or professional development sessions. If done like this, MTSS remains a separate initiative, something staff members "get through" rather than something they live and breathe. Now, contrast that with a school where MTSS is embedded into everything:

- The morning announcements reinforce SEL strategies, reminding students of calming techniques before a big test.

- Teachers use data daily, reviewing student progress and adjusting instruction as needed, not just waiting for quarterly benchmarks or universal screeners.
- Collaboration isn't an occasional MTSS meeting; it's scheduled. Grade-level teams discuss student data in their weekly PLC meetings to ensure no student falls through the cracks.
- Administrators talk about MTSS principles in every staff meeting, reinforcing that MTSS is not a side project; it's the way they do school.

If MTSS only shows up in meetings and not in daily routines, it is not culture. It's compliance.

MTSS requires intentional shifts in the way adults think, collaborate, and respond to student needs, and this shift is not optional. It is a readiness condition. MTSS is about adults taking ownership of their impact on student outcomes. When educators recognize their role in creating equitable learning environments, they shift from reacting to problems to proactively preventing them.

MTSS demands more than new tools or additional meetings. It requires adults to examine long-standing practices, question habits that feel familiar, and address inconsistencies that have been normalized over time. This is often the hardest part of the work. Not because educators don't care, but because change requires confronting what we control, not just what students do.

If expectations vary widely from classroom to classroom, your culture is not ready.
If data is reviewed but not acted upon, your culture is not ready.

If accountability depends on who is leading the meeting that day, your culture is not ready.

These are not implementation issues. They are readiness issues.

To recap, MTSS does not expose student deficits first. It exposes adult misalignment. It reveals where collaboration is surface-level, where routines lack consistency, and where leadership has tolerated variation in the name of flexibility. A system can appear busy and still be unprepared.

So before you move forward into deeper planning, pause and ask yourself:

Are we aligned in expectation and practice?
Are we willing to address inconsistencies when we see it?
Are we prepared to hold ourselves accountable at the same level we hold our students?

CHAPTER 4

The 5-Step Process for Building Readiness

One of the biggest mistakes schools make with implementation is jumping straight into the implementation phase without proper planning. While it's tempting to dive straight into the "nuts and bolts" of MTSS, a solid foundation is essential for success. Building an MTSS framework takes time, intentionality, and collaboration. According to Fixsen et al., (2005), the planning and implementation stages alone can take upwards of four years to ensure all the pieces are in place. Yes, you read that correctly…four years. Getting to full MTSS implementation is not a one-time event; it's an ongoing process, but this process must begin with proper planning and preparation. In this chapter, we will explore a 5-step process for planning an MTSS framework that lays the groundwork for sustainable success.

This Is Not a Linear Checklist

Before we move into the five steps, there is something I need to make absolutely clear.

This is not a checklist.

It may be presented as a sequence, but it is not meant to be completed, checked off, and left behind. If that is how this process is approached, the system will move forward with the appearance of readiness, but without the substance to sustain it.

Readiness is not always linear; it does not happen in a straight line.

In practice, schools and districts do not move cleanly from Step 1 to Step 5 and then arrive at implementation fully prepared. What actually happens can be far less orderly and a bit messy at times. As teams revisit earlier steps, or as new information arises that requires rethinking of previous decisions, assumptions that felt solid at the beginning begin to shift as the work becomes more visible. And that is OK because that is a sign that the system is engaging in real readiness work.

For example, a district may complete a needs assessment and determine that MTSS is both necessary and feasible. Leadership teams are formed, essential components are identified, and a self-assessment is conducted. On paper, the system appears ready to move forward. But once teams really begin examining their data more closely or attempting to align practices across schools, they may realize that their initial assumptions about capacity or alignment were incomplete.

At that point, the system has two choices.

It can continue moving forward in the sequence because it feels like progress, or it can pause and step back to earlier steps to address what has now been uncovered. But this is where many systems begin to drift away from readiness.

They drift because they feel obligated to keep moving. There is this belief that going back means losing time. In reality, moving forward without addressing what has been revealed creates far more strain later in the process. What was overlooked at the beginning does not just go away; it shows up during implementation, when the cost of addressing it is significantly higher.

This is why readiness cannot be treated as a one-time phase. It must be approached as an ongoing, iterative process.

The steps in this chapter are meant to guide your thinking, not rush actions. These two things are connected though. What is learned in one step should influence the others. The needs assessment informs team structure. Team structure influences how the essential components are defined. The essential components shape how the self-assessment is interpreted. The self-assessment drives action planning. And action planning, when done well, often reveals the need to revisit earlier decisions. This is the work. This is the readiness work.

Systems that approach readiness as a one-time phase tend to move quickly into implementation, but they struggle to operationalize. Systems that approach readiness as an ongoing process build the capacity to adjust, refine, and sustain the work over time.

But here is another reality that leaders must recognize.

Different parts of the system will not move at the same pace. One school may demonstrate strong alignment in instruction but struggle with data use. Another may have clear structures in place but lack consistency in practice. A district may have a well-defined leadership team but limited capacity at the building level. Readiness is not achieved when one area is strong. It is achieved when the system, as a whole, is aligned enough to function consistently.

But what is "enough"? We're not looking for perfection here. Enough is when the system can operate predictably without relying on individual effort to hold it together.

It means instruction is consistent enough across all classrooms that it doesn't matter which teacher's classroom students are placed in. It means intervention is structured enough that students receive the support they truly need when they need it. It means data is used consistently enough that instructional decisions are not left to interpretation. And it means leadership is aligned enough that expectations do not shift depending on who is communicating them.

"Enough" is when variability is no longer the defining feature of the system.

Will there still be areas for growth? Yes. Will there still be inconsistencies? Yes. But those inconsistencies are no longer systemic; they're not impacting the overall performance of the system. They are identifiable and addressable.

In other words, the system is stable. Teams know what to do. They know when to do it. The work does not depend on a few individuals doing it well; it is supported by structures that make consistency possible across the system.

That is what "enough" looks like. And if the system cannot operate that way yet, then the readiness work is not complete.

Leaders must be willing to hold multiple realities at once. Progress in one area does not eliminate the need for growth in another. Movement forward does not mean the system is ready. It means the system is in motion. And motion is not the same as readiness.

If you take anything from this section, let it be this: Readiness is not something you complete one time and you're done. It is something you build, revisit, and strengthen over time.

The steps that follow will help provide structure for that work. But the effectiveness of those steps depends on how they are used. If they are treated as tasks to finish, the system will move forward without the alignment it needs. If they are used as a framework for reflection and decision-making, they will help you build a system that is not only prepared to implement MTSS, but capable of sustaining it.
So as you move into Step 1, resist the urge to rush.
Pay attention to what the work is revealing.
And be willing to pause when the system is not yet ready to move forward.
Because in this process, slowing down doesn't mean delay.
It means you're building a strong foundation that will make everything else possible.

Step 1: Conduct a Needs Assessment

The first step in planning an MTSS framework is determining whether the initiative is both needed and feasible for your district or organization. This requires a thorough needs assessment. This is quite different from a self-assessment, which we'll talk about later. The purpose of doing this initial exploring with the needs assessment, is to assess whether the school and/or district's needs match the proposed initiative and to then make a decision as to whether it should proceed or not (Fixsen, et. al., 2005; Metz & Louison, 2019). A needs assessment answers questions like: *Is this the right time to implement this initiative? Is this something we can manage at this time? Do we have the capacity to take this on right now?*

When conducting a needs assessment, stakeholders, including the superintendent (or designee), their cabinet, and any other pertinent officials meet to: discuss the implications of adopting MTSS (or any other initiative), assess whether the district has the resources, time, and capacity to implement MTSS effectively, and evaluate current district priorities and any ongoing initiatives that might conflict with or complement MTSS. For example, districts undergoing major restructuring or referendums may not have the capacity to take on a new initiative and may decide that implementing a new initiative is not feasible at this time. To help with the discussion, tools such as the hexagon tool are great to use to help facilitate this process (Metz & Louison, 2019). A thorough needs assessment ensures that districts embark on the MTSS journey intentionally, with the readiness to succeed.

What a Weak vs. Strong Needs Assessment Actually Looks Like

At this point, it is important to pause and make a distinction that is often overlooked. Not all needs assessments are the same. In many systems (if they even conduct one), the needs assessment is just a formality. It is conducted because it is expected, not because it is used to make a real decision. Teams gather, discuss the initiative, and ultimately move forward with implementation because the assumption has already been made that MTSS (or whatever initiative) is the right next step.
That is not a needs assessment. That's more of a confirmation process.

A weak needs assessment is focused on whether MTSS is a good idea. A strong needs assessment is focused on whether the system is prepared to sustain it. Those are two very different angles. In a weak needs assessment, the conversation centers around the benefits of MTSS. Leaders discuss how it can improve student outcomes, align supports, and create a more structured approach to intervention. While these points are valid, they do not determine readiness. The decision to move forward is often influenced by other factors such as state expectations, district trends, the desire to keep pace with other systems, or some higher-up's unilateral decision to do so. And since the decision to move forward has already been made, critical realities can go unchallenged or unaddressed.

Competing initiatives may be acknowledged but not addressed. Capacity is assumed rather than evaluated. Timing is treated as flexible, even when the system is already under strain. The system moves forward not because it is ready, but because it feels like it has to.
And when that happens, the gap has already been created.

A strong needs assessment looks very different. It is not centered on whether MTSS is valuable or not. That has already been established. Instead, it is centered on whether the system, as it currently operates, can take on the work without creating fragmentation. It requires leaders to face realities and ask more difficult questions, like: Is this the right time for this work, given everything else the system is carrying"? Do we have the capacity–not just in staffing, but in time, focus, and leadership attention–to support this implementation with consistency? Are our current systems stable enough to integrate MTSS, or will this become another layer added to an already fragmented structure? What will need to stop, shift, or be deprioritized in order for this work to be done well? These are not comfortable questions, but they are necessary ones. A strong needs assessment does not assume readiness.

It tests for it.

In systems where the needs assessment process is taken seriously, the outcome is not always a green light to move forward immediately. In some cases, the most strategic decision is to delay implementation. Not because MTSS is not needed, but because the system is not yet positioned to sustain it. That decision requires discipline. It requires leaders to prioritize long-term success over short-term action. It requires acknowledging that moving forward too soon will create more work later, not less. And it requires the willingness to say, "Not yet," even when there is pressure to act.

But what if the pressure is coming from a state mandate, and you don't have the option to opt out and say, "not yet"? What if the work is not a choice, but a expected requirement? In these cases, leaders are not deciding whether to implement the initiative; that decision has already been made at the state level. So, the question is no longer *if* the system will move forward with the initiative, but *how*.

Even when implementation is mandated, the need for readiness does not change.

The approach does.

When a school district receives a mandate, the first thing they usually do is jump straight into trying to implement it. They attempt to jump in while simultaneously trying to build the foundation. That is one of the biggest mistakes I've seen school district systems make. That is where strain is created, and right there is the beginning of a fractured system. Instead, leaders must differentiate between compliance and capacity-building. Compliance may require some immediate action because there is a state mandate. But capacity-building is what determines whether those actions will be sustained.

Even within a mandate, district and school leaders can still control some key decisions:
They can control how quickly the work is scaled.
They can control how expectations are communicated.
They can control the approach.
Leadership has the choice in deciding whether the system should focus on just getting the work done now, or on whether they should first build the foundational capacity needed to keep the work going over time.

Yes, a mandate may require you to do some immediate actions, but those actions do not have to be rushed. It does not mean that you have to skip the work of building alignment, capacity, and coherence. It does not remove the responsibility of building the system intentionally.

So the question becomes, "How do we move forward without compromising the foundation?"

Strong leaders move forward where they must, but they are also intentional about where they slow down. They protect time for alignment. They build capacity alongside early implementation. They resist the urge to quickly expand before the system can function consistently. They meet the requirement. But they do not abandon the work of readiness to do so. They still dedicate time to building a foundation. Because even under a mandate, the outcome remains the same: improving student outcomes. Systems that include readiness while moving forward sustain the work. Systems that ignore readiness in the name of urgency spend far more time repairing their systems in the long run.

Another characteristic of a strong needs assessment is that it brings clarity to what readiness will require. It identifies where the system is aligned and where it is not. It surfaces gaps in leadership alignment, capacity, and competing priorities before those gaps show up during implementation. It makes the invisible visible. And that is the whole point, to see or acknowledge, what was not seen before.

The purpose of a needs assessment is not to justify the work. It is to determine whether the system can carry the work. If that question is not being answered honestly, then the process has not served its purpose. And if the process has not served its purpose, then the system is already moving forward without readiness.

As you reflect on your own context, think about this: Did your needs assessment just confirm a decision that had already been made? Or did it actually challenge your system to determine whether it was truly ready to move forward? Because the difference between those two approaches is not procedural. It is the difference between building a system that can sustain the work and one that will struggle to maintain it.

Step 2: Build Your District and School Leadership Teams

Once the need has been established, the next step is assembling a *district-level* MTSS leadership team. This team serves as the backbone of the framework, driving consistent and effective implementation across the district. The team may include: a district MTSS coordinator/director, behavior coach, social workers, director of assessment, reading specialist, and other relevant district-level leaders. It is important for the MTSS coordinator/director (or whoever will be leading the implementation at the district level) to have autonomy and decision-making authority. This ensures that the work is not stalled and doesn't have to wait on "higher-ups" to keep the work moving.

The district-level team will be responsible for: aligning the district's MTSS framework with broader organizational goals, designing policies, data systems, and intervention protocols to support implementation, planning and organizing professional development to build staff capacity effectively, and ensuring equitable allocation of resources across all schools within the district. Here's why this matters: it ensures that MTSS is not just treated as an isolated program but as a unified system embedded in the district's culture. This team will provide the vision, structure, and accountability needed for successful implementation across the board.

Each school should also have a dedicated MTSS team. This team will need to consist of members from the school such as a decision-maker (Principal or Assistant Principal), interventionist, instructional coach, teachers, behavior specialist, and school counselor. Also, other support members such as the speech-language pathologist, special education teacher, or other specialist could also be a member of the school team. This team is ultimately responsible for making sure the overall implementation of MTSS is healthy at the school level.

Decision-Making Authority: Who Owns What

At this point in the process, many systems believe they are ready to move forward because they have established teams. Just because you've identified the team doesn't mean there is clarity amongst it. And if there is no clarity, the work will surely stall.

One of the most common breakdowns in MTSS implementation is not a lack of effort or even a lack of understanding. It is the lack of clearly defined decision-making authority and who owns what. Yes, teams are in place, and meetings are happening. There might even be some rich conversations taking place. But when it is time to make decisions, there is hesitation.

Who decides?
Who owns the outcome?
Who is responsible for follow-through?
When those questions are not clearly answered, the system defaults to hesitation. Decisions are delayed. Ownership becomes shared in name but absent in practice. And over time, the work loses momentum.
This is a readiness issue.
Why? Because a system cannot function consistently if the people within it are unclear about what they are responsible for and what they are empowered to decide.

At the district level, leadership is responsible for setting direction. This includes establishing the vision for MTSS, defining non-negotiables, aligning the work to broader priorities, and ensuring that the necessary structures and resources are in place. District leadership determines what must be consistent across all schools and what flexibility can exist at the building level. Without that clarity, schools are left to interpret expectations on their own. Systems are not supposed to rely on interpretation. They're supposed to rely on consistency. When people have to interpret expectations on their own, they fill in the gaps based on their own experiences, beliefs, and comfort level. And this is where interpretation can lead to variability. That means the same expectation gets carried out in different ways across classrooms, teams, or schools.

At the school level, leadership is responsible for execution. This includes ensuring that the structures defined at the district level are implemented with consistency, that staff understand expectations, and that practices are monitored and adjusted as needed. School leaders are not simply participants in MTSS; they are responsible for ensuring that it functions as part of the daily operation of the building. But when that responsibility is unclear or inconsistently exercised, implementation becomes uneven. For example, some schools may move forward with clarity and consistency while others struggle to translate expectations into practice. That's not a system. That is a collection of different approaches operating under the name of MTSS, when it's really not.

Here's what effective MTSS teams do. Effective teams operate with clarity around who facilitates, who brings data, who guides problem-solving, and who is responsible for ensuring that decisions are implemented and followed through. Without that clarity, meetings become conversations rather than decision-making spaces. And conversations, no matter how productive they feel, do not move the work forward if they do not lead to action.

There is also a distinction that must be made between participation and ownership. Many individuals may participate in MTSS processes. Fewer are responsible for ensuring that those processes lead to consistent outcomes. Readiness requires identifying who owns the work at each level of the system and ensuring that ownership is understood, accepted, and supported.

Because if ownership is unclear, accountability becomes inconsistent. And when accountability is inconsistent, expectations become optional.

This is where systems begin to drift.

Leaders may believe that the work is being carried out because structures are in place and meetings are happening. But without clear authority and ownership, those structures cannot function as intended. They rely on individual initiative rather than system design. And anything that relies on individual initiative will eventually break down. When people understand their roles, collaboration becomes more focused. Decisions are made without ambiguity. Follow-through is expected and monitored. The system begins to operate with consistency because it is no longer dependent on interpretation.

So as you consider your own system, ask yourself:
Is it clear who makes decisions at the district level?
Is it clear who is responsible for implementation at the school level?
Is it clear who owns the work within your teams?
If the answer to any of these questions is unclear, then the system is not yet ready to move forward with implementation.

Clarity of ownership is a readiness condition that determines whether the work will move forward or stall.

And when the work stalls, the system doesn't just pause—it starts to fall apart.

Step 3: Identify and Norm on Essential Components

What are essential components? Essential components are the foundational elements or building blocks that define the *what* and *how* of your MTSS implementation framework. The essential components are important because they tell us *what* is essential–the non-negotiables. Then, the processes, framework, or system that we create will define and tell us the *how*. These components provide the structure and clarity needed to guide the MTSS implementation work. Keep in mind that since MTSS is a framework, the essential components can be customized to fit your school or district's needs. And when customizing your components, please understand that the components can vary from one district to another, or from state to state. Districts should determine their own components (if there are no state-adopted ones) based upon their unique needs and priorities. Here are some common essential components found within MTSS frameworks that I have seen: *leadership, communication and collaboration, capacity building, problem-solving, tiered systems, and data evaluation.*

From Agreement to Consistency

By this point in the process, most systems have done something important. They have named what matters. They have identified their essential components. Teams have come together, and there is a sense of alignment in conversation. People are able to articulate the focus. There is agreement around what the work should look like. And on the surface, that feels like progress, right? This is where many systems overestimate their readiness. They think that just because they have agreed on a few things up until this point, their system is now cohesive.

Let me share something: agreement is not the same as consistency.
It is one thing for a team to agree on essential components in a meeting. It is another thing entirely for those components to show up the same way across classrooms, across teams, and across buildings. Consistency, not agreement, is where the real work begins.
Agreement lives in conversation.
Consistency lives in practice.
And the gap between the two is where many systems struggle.

It is possible to have strong agreement around instruction and still see wide variation in how that instruction is delivered. It is possible to agree that data should drive decisions and still see teams interpreting and using data in completely different ways. It is possible to agree on intervention structures and still have students experiencing very different levels of support depending on where they are. When that happens, the system is not aligned. It is loosely connected in name, but not in practice. And loosely connected systems do not produce consistent outcomes. This is why essential components cannot remain solely at the level of agreement. They must be translated into clear expectations for practice.

What does this look like in action?
It means that when a component such as "data-driven decision-making" is named as an essential component, the system defines what that actually looks like in practice. Not in general terms, but in observable practice. What data will be used? Who is responsible for getting the data? How often will it be reviewed? What decisions should follow? What does it look like when this is happening well, and what does it look like when it is not?

The same is true for instruction, intervention, and collaboration. If expectations are not clearly defined, they will be interpreted. And when they are interpreted, they will vary. That variation may not feel significant at first. In fact, it is sometimes justified as flexibility. But over time, it becomes the reason the system cannot function consistently. Students receive different experiences. Teams operate differently. Outcomes become unpredictable. And once again, the system is carrying variability instead of stability.

The goal is consistency across the board, not variability.

Now, some may ask, "What's wrong with everyone doing things differently if we're all working toward the same goal?"

Here's the issue.

When everyone is doing something different, even with the best intentions, the system loses its ability to function predictably. Students begin to experience different expectations, different levels of support, and different instructional approaches depending on where they are. At that point, outcomes are no longer tied to student need. They are tied to variability in practice. And we can't effectively measure the impact of those individual efforts if they're all doing things differently. Individual efforts, no matter how strong they are, do not produce consistent outcomes across a school or district. Because what happens when that person leaves?

Let me be clear. Consistency does not mean that every classroom looks identical or that professional judgment is removed. It means that there are shared expectations for how the work is carried out. It means that when a student moves from one classroom to another, they are still experiencing the same level of clarity, the same instructional priorities, and the same approach to support. Without that level of consistency, the system cannot reliably deliver results. So the goal is not for everyone to do the same thing in a rigid way.
The goal is for everyone to operate within the same system.

This is where leadership becomes critical. Leaders are responsible for moving the system to consistency. That requires more than facilitating conversations. It requires establishing clear expectations, monitoring how those expectations are carried out, and addressing inconsistencies when they appear. This is the part of the work that is often avoided. Not because leaders do not understand its importance, but because it requires sustained attention. It requires follow-through. It requires having tough conversations when practices do not align with expectations.

If a system is serious about readiness, it must be willing to examine whether its essential components are actually being implemented with consistency. Not in isolated pockets, but across the entire system. Because readiness is not demonstrated by what the system says it values. It is demonstrated by what the system does repeatedly.

So the question is not, "Do we agree on our essential components"? The question is, "Are those components showing up the same way, in the same conditions, across our system?"

If the answer is no, then the work is not complete. And until agreement becomes consistency, the system is not yet ready to sustain implementation.

Step 4: Conduct a Self-Assessment

After establishing essential components, the next step is evaluating readiness through a self-assessment. Unlike the needs assessment, which determines feasibility, the self-assessment measures current practices and identifies system strengths and gaps. The self-assessment provides a snapshot of where the district currently stands in terms of MTSS implementation, strengths and barriers, and alignment with the essential components. The self-assessment provides actionable insights to inform the next steps in the planning process.

Here's how to conduct the self-assessment: Have school MTSS teams complete the self-assessment to evaluate their practices, using a reliable instrument or tool, such as the Self-Assessment of MTSS

(SAM)(National Center on Intensive Intervention, 2017). For the best and most accurate results, ensure that the directions for the instrument are followed with fidelity. Then, analyze the results to identify areas requiring additional support, resources, or professional development. But how do you accurately interpret the results? Let's discuss that next.

How to Interpret Results Without Minimizing the Truth

At this stage, your district or school has taken a closer look at itself by conducting the self-assessment. Data has been gathered. Ratings have been assigned. On paper, there is now a clearer picture of where the system stands. But this is where another critical shift must happen.
Just collecting the data is not the work. Interpreting it honestly is. And this is where many systems begin to lose clarity. Not because the data is unclear, but because of how it is interpreted.

here is a natural tendency to soften what the data reveals. Teams look at areas of weakness and immediately try to explain them. Context is added. Exceptions are highlighted. Progress is emphasized, even when consistency is not yet present. I heard things said such as,

"We're working on that."
"We've started to see some improvement."
"That's not true across every grade level."
All of those statements may be accurate. But they can also become a way of avoiding the central issue. The purpose of a self-assessment is not to defend the system. It is to understand it. And understanding requires honesty.

A rating of "developing" does not mean the system is almost there. It means the practice is not yet consistent. A rating of "partially in place" does not mean the system is ready to move forward. It means there are some gaps that will affect implementation if they are not addressed.

When those distinctions are minimized, the system begins to operate on a false sense of readiness. And false readiness is one of the most dangerous conditions when implementing an initiative. It creates movement, but no stability. And this is how systems move forward believing they are prepared, only to encounter breakdowns down the line that could have been avoided.

Another common misstep is treating all findings as equal. Not every gap carries the same weight. Some areas of growth will not significantly impact the system's ability to function. Others will.
For example, a lack of consistency in instructional practice will have a far greater impact on implementation than a minor gap in documentation. If everything is treated as a priority, nothing becomes a priority. And when that happens, action plans become overloaded, focus becomes diluted, and the system struggles to gain traction. Interpreting results requires discernment. It requires identifying which gaps are foundational and which are secondary. It requires understanding which conditions must be strengthened before the system can move forward with confidence. And it requires the discipline to focus.

There is also a tendency to view the self-assessment as a reflection point rather than a decision point. But this is not just a moment to reflect. It is a moment to decide. Based on what the data reveals, what is the system actually ready to do? Not what it hopes to do. Not what it feels pressured to do. What is it saying the system is actually ready to do with consistency? That question matters because it determines the next phase of the work.

As we've alluded to previously in this book, if the system moves forward without addressing foundational gaps, those gaps will show up again during implementation, often with greater impact. What could have been addressed early becomes more difficult to correct later. This is why interpretation must lead to prioritization. And prioritization must lead to disciplined action.

Not everything can be addressed at once. And attempting to do so will bog the system down rather than move it forward. Strong systems identify a small number of high-leverage areas and commit to strengthening them with focus and consistency. Depth creates stability, and stability creates the conditions for expansion.

So as you review your own self-assessment results, resist the urge to soften what you see. Resist the urge to explain it away. And resist the urge to move forward too quickly.

Instead, ask:
What is this data actually telling us about how our system operates?
Where are we inconsistent in ways that will impact implementation?
What must be strengthened before we move forward?
Because the accuracy of your answers will determine the effectiveness of your next steps.

Step 5: Create an Action Plan

The final step in planning is translating insights from the needs and self-assessments into a concrete action plan. Action plans bring clarity, accountability, and structure to the MTSS process and ensure that planning translates into measurable and sustainable progress. An action plan outlines: improvement goals–specific targets based on self-assessment findings; roles and responsibilities–clear assignments for who will "own" each action; timelines–deadlines for completing tasks and milestones for progress checks; and resources–plans for securing materials, programs, or training. Examples of action planning next steps might include: developing a professional development cadence to build staff capacity; purchasing evidence-based intervention programs (e.g., Delta RTI, Bridges, UFLI, etc.); defining roles and responsibilities for Tier 2 and Tier 3 interventions; and creating an MTSS guidance document to house best practices and implementation protocols. But even after the best planning intentions, action plans can still fall short. Let's talk about why.

Why Most Action Plans Fail

By the time systems reach this step, there is often a sense of momentum. The needs have been identified. Teams are in place. Essential components have been normed on, and the system has been self-assessed. Plans are written. Goals are outlined. Timelines are established. Documents are created that reflect thoughtful effort and clear intention. But despite all of that, many action plans fail to produce meaningful change. Not because the plan was poorly written. But because it's trying to do too much. Too many priorities. Too many goals. Too many actions happening all at the same time. All of this looks good on paper, but in practice, it becomes unmanageable.

When everything is the focus, nothing is. The efforts have increase, but the impact has not.

And when impact does not follow effort, frustration sets in.

Another issue is lack of alignment. Action plans are often created as standalone documents rather than as extensions of the system's readiness needs. Goals may be well-intentioned, but they are not always tied to the most critical gaps identified in the self-assessment. Or they are written in ways that do not directly influence daily practice. If the system is not changing the way it operates, the action plan becomes just a piece of paper.

Another reason action plans fail is due to a lack of clarity around ownership. When responsibilities are not clearly defined, implementation breaks down. When responsibility is assigned broadly, accountability becomes unclear. Teams may assume the work will get done, but without a clear owner and a mechanism to ensure follow-through, it rarely does. And what is not clearly owned is rarely sustained.

Another common issue is the absence of follow-through. Plans are created, but they are not revisited with consistency or discipline. Progress is not actively monitored, and adjustments are not made based on what the system is learning. Over time, the plan becomes a document that lives in a binder rather than a tool that drives the work. And when that happens, the work becomes disconnected from the plan that was meant to guide it.

When a system is implementing a plan, decisions are intentional. There is a defined focus, clear priorities, and agreed-upon actions that guide the work. The system knows what it is trying to accomplish and how it is going to get there. But when follow-through breaks down, that structure disappears. Instead of acting on a plan, the system starts responding to whatever is happening in the moment. Urgent issues take priority. New ideas get introduced without alignment. Attention shifts based on immediate needs rather than long-term goals. At that point, the work is no longer guided. It's reacting. And reactive systems struggle to sustain change because they are constantly adjusting to circumstances rather than building consistency over time. Even a well-written plan cannot produce results if it is not actively guiding decisions and actions.

What Makes an Action Plan Executable

An effective action plan is not defined by how many pages it is. It's defined by whether or not the system can execute the plan consistently. Strong systems do not try to solve everything at once. They identify a small number of high-leverage priorities and commit to addressing them deeply. They understand that narrowing the focus increases the likelihood of consistent implementation.

Clarity is also essential.

Each action within the plan must be specific enough that it can be carried out without interpretation. What is being done? Who is responsible? When will it happen? What does successful implementation look like? If these questions cannot be answered clearly, the action will vary in practice. And variation weakens execution.

Ownership must also be explicit. Every action should have a clearly identified owner who is responsible for ensuring that it happens. Not a general role. A specific individual who is accountable for follow-through. Because accountability does not exist in ambiguity.

Monitoring is another critical component. An executable plan is not set and left alone. It is revisited regularly. Progress is examined. Data is used to determine whether the actions are producing the intended outcomes. When they are not, adjustments are made. This creates a feedback loop between planning and implementation. And that loop is what allows the system to refine its work over time.

Finally, an executable plan is aligned to the system's readiness. It does not push implementation beyond what the system can sustain. It builds capacity while the work is happening, strengthening the foundation as new practices are introduced. That way, the system is able to absorb and carry the work. When a plan exceeds the system's capacity, it will break down--every time.

So as you develop your action plan, resist the urge to make it overly broad. Focus on what matters most--making it executable. Define it clearly. Assign ownership. Monitor it consistently. And align it to what your system is actually ready to carry. The strength of your plan is not measured by what it includes. It is measured by what your system can do, repeatedly, over time.

Planning for MTSS isn't about checking boxes or rushing to implement. It's about laying a strong foundation and properly preparing your system to ensure success for all involved. By following this 5-step process, districts can create a framework that not only supports students but also transforms systems and empowers educators. Thoughtful planning today leads to impactful change tomorrow. And if you start with clarity and build with purpose, the system you design today will become the support structure your students can depend on tomorrow.

The Readiness Reality Check

Here is a moment to pause. Not to review what has been completed, but to examine what is actually true about how your system operates. Because by this point, it is possible to *feel* ready just because your system has followed the steps.

On paper, the system may appear prepared to move into implementation. But readiness is not determined on paper. It is revealed in practice. And this is where many systems move forward too soon.

Before moving into the next phase, the question is not, "Have we completed the steps"?

The question is, "Can our system carry this work with consistency?" That question must be answered honestly.

If instruction varies significantly from one classroom to another, the system is not ready.

If roles and responsibilities are still unclear or inconsistently executed, the system is not ready.

If data is being collected but not consistently used to drive decisions, the system is not ready.

If expectations shift depending on the person, the meeting, or the situation, the system is not ready.

These are indicators that the system cannot yet function with the level of predictability required to sustain MTSS.

And when systems move forward under those conditions, implementation becomes harder than it needs to be. What could have been established during readiness must now be corrected during implementation. Clarity has to be built, or rebuilt, while the right work is already underway. If alignment has to be created under pressure, that is where strain begins.

But, this does not mean the system has failed. It means the system has to make a decision.

Will we move forward because we *feel* ready? Or will we move forward because the system has demonstrated that it is ready? Those are not the same.

Demonstrated readiness is visible. It shows up in consistent practice, not isolated examples. It shows up in shared understanding that translates into action. It shows up in systems that operate with enough predictability that the work does not depend on individual effort to hold it together.

That is the standard. Consistency.

So as you prepare to move beyond this point, do not rush past this moment. Use it.

Look closely at how your system is actually functioning. Identify where variability still exists. Be honest about what the system can and cannot yet sustain.

The strength of your implementation will always be limited by the strength of your readiness. Implementation cannot outperform the system it sits on, if readiness work is not the foundation.

No matter how strong the plan is, how much training is provided, or how committed people are, the results will only be as strong as the system's ability to carry the work consistently.

If readiness is weak – if instruction is inconsistent, roles are unclear, data isn't driving decisions, or leadership is not aligned – those conditions will limit what implementation can achieve. The work may start, but it will require constant correction, added support, and ongoing repair.

So the ceiling of your implementation is set before implementation even begins.

If the system is not ready to operate with consistency, implementation will not fix that.

It will only expose it.

CHAPTER 5

Tools That Tell You the Truth About Readiness

Let's pause for a moment.

By now, you understand that MTSS isn't a checklist; it's a culture, a commitment. You've seen how skipping over readiness can lead to frustration, burnout, and initiative fatigue. So, here's the natural next question you should be asking: How do we actually assess and build readiness in a way that's clear, strategic, and real?

That's what this chapter is about.

Readiness isn't something you "feel." It's a system. And systems need tools. Tools that help you lead with precision, assess with honesty, and build with intention. Having the right tools in place helps you pause, reflect, calibrate, and course-correct before you leap into implementation.

What Your Tools Aren't Telling You

Before we begin working through specific tools, there is something that needs to be addressed. Not all tools are created for the same purpose. In fact, many of the tools used in MTSS implementation were never designed to tell the truth about a system. They were designed to document activity, demonstrate compliance, or provide a general sense of progress. And because of that, they often give leaders a false sense of confidence about where their system actually stands.

This is the distinction between **compliance tools** and **diagnostic tools**.

Compliance tools are designed to answer the question: *"Are we doing what we said we would do"?*

Diagnostic tools are designed to answer a very different question: *"Is our system actually functioning in a way that will produce results"?*

These are two totally different things, and that difference matters. A compliance tool might tell you that data meetings are happening. A diagnostic tool will tell you whether those meetings are producing decisions that impact instruction.

A compliance tool might confirm that interventions are scheduled. A diagnostic tool will reveal whether those interventions are aligned to students' needs and connected to Tier 1 instruction.

Compliance tools track activity. Diagnostic tools examine effectiveness.

And in systems where readiness has not been fully established, relying on compliance tools creates one of the most dangerous conditions in implementation: the illusion that the system is further along than it actually is. This is where many leaders unintentionally misread their system.

Because on paper, everything appears to be in place. So the conclusion becomes: *"We're doing fine."* But when a system is evaluated primarily through compliance measures, it is very easy to generate what can be described as **false positives**. False positives occur when the system appears healthy based on surface-level indicators, while deeper inconsistencies remain unaddressed.

For example, a school may report that all grade levels are meeting regularly to review data. That is a positive indicator. But if each grade level team is interpreting data differently, applying different criteria for decision-making, or leaving meetings without clear action steps, then the system is not functioning consistently. The tool confirmed that meetings occurred, but it did not reveal whether the meetings were effective. In this way, the tool did not provide clarity. It provided comfort. And comfort, when it is not grounded in truth, slows progress.

Another limitation of many tools is that they lack specificity. They ask broad questions that invite broad answers. Questions such as:

- "Do teachers use data to inform instruction?"
- "Is Tier 1 instruction effective?"
- "Are interventions implemented with fidelity?"

While these questions may seem useful, they leave too much room for interpretation. What does "use data" actually look like in practice? What defines "effective" instruction? How do you define "fidelity" across different classrooms?

Without clear, observable indicators, different individuals will answer the same question based on their own perception, experience, or expectation. One leader may interpret "effective instruction" as alignment to standards, while another interprets it as student engagement. One team may define "fidelity" as following a schedule, while another defines it as adherence to instructional routines.

When this happens, the tool is not measuring consistency; it's measuring perception. And perception is not sufficient for determining readiness.

Finally, many tools fail because they do not drive decisions. They are completed, reviewed, and sometimes even discussed, but they are not used to determine what happens next. Results are summarized rather than analyzed. Data is acknowledged rather than acted upon. The process ends with completion instead of continuation.

In these cases, the tool becomes an event rather than a mechanism for change. Leaders may walk away with general insights, but without clear implications for action:

- What needs to stop?
- What needs to be strengthened?
- What is not yet ready?
- What should not move forward?

If a tool does not help answer these questions, it is not functioning as a readiness tool. It is functioning as documentation.

This is why the purpose of tools in this work must be redefined. Tools are not meant to confirm that the system is on track. They are meant to reveal where the system is not yet ready. They are not meant to provide reassurance. They are meant to provide clarity. And clarity is not always comfortable.

In fact, the most effective readiness tools will often surface misalignment, inconsistency, and gaps that have been operating beneath the surface. They will highlight differences in practice across classrooms, discrepancies in how teams make decisions, and areas where leadership expectations have not been fully established or reinforced.

As you move through the tools in this chapter, do not approach them as just a way to check your progress. Approach them as a way to see your system clearly.

Not as you hope it is.
Not as it appears on paper.
But as it actually operates.

Your decisions are only as strong as what you can clearly see. And when used correctly, tools are what make that visibility possible.

A strong MTSS framework is only as effective as the tools that support its planning, monitoring, and improvement. While MTSS is a mindset and a system, it also depends on practical, everyday tools that help schools turn intention into action. Let's start with tools that assess how ready schools are to begin implementation of MTSS, or any initiative.

Tools for Assessing Readiness

1. MTSS Readiness Checklist

This is your flashlight in the dark. Before you launch, pause and ask*:* Are we actually ready to do this work well? An MTSS Readiness Checklist includes indicators related to leadership commitment, team formation, data systems, and resource allocation. It provides a reality check and highlights areas that need strengthening before launching MTSS practices.

This checklist helps you uncover your blind spots before they become system-wide frustrations down the road. Research on implementation science consistently emphasizes that organizational readiness –including leadership alignment, staff capacity, and infrastructure– is one of the strongest predictors of successful implementation. Schools that assess readiness before implementation are significantly more likely to sustain MTSS practices and avoid the cycle of initiative fatigue.

Readiness Predicts Implementation Success

Implementation research consistently shows that initiatives fail far less often because of the framework itself and far more often because organizations begin implementation before key readiness conditions are established.

A multi-year study examining schools implementing MTSS-related frameworks found that schools with strong leadership alignment, clear implementation teams, and structured planning tools were significantly more likely to sustain practices and improve student outcomes compared to schools that rushed into implementation without those structures.

In other words, the difference between schools that struggle and schools that succeed often comes down to whether readiness was assessed before implementation began.

Readiness Reflection: Are you building your MTSS on sand instead of a solid foundation?

2. Needs Assessment Tool

While the readiness checklist looks internally, the needs assessment zooms out. This tool helps district leaders ask: Is this the right time for this initiative? Do we have the capacity? Is this aligned with our strategic goals—or are we just jumping on a trend? This tool is best used at the district leadership level when deciding how to adopt or expand an initiative such as MTSS, especially if schools are juggling multiple initiatives. Research examining district-level MTSS implementation has shown that misalignment between initiatives and organizational priorities is a major contributor to implementation failure (Forman et al., 2020). Districts that conduct structured needs assessments are more likely to implement MTSS strategically rather than reactively, ensuring that initiatives align with existing goals, resources, and instructional priorities.

Needs assessments also help districts identify systemic barriers before implementation begins, allowing leaders to proactively address issues related to staffing, professional learning, and data infrastructure.

Readiness Reflection: Does the timing and context support implementation success, or are we setting ourselves up for initiative overload?

Next, let's look at tools that help lay the foundation for implementation success.

Tools That Build the Blueprint

3. Essential Components Norming Guide

You can't implement what you haven't defined. As mentioned earlier, the essential components set the norms for how you plan to implement MTSS in your school or district. While each district should define its own essential components, the essential components norming guide offers a structured way to evaluate how well those components are defined, communicated, embedded, and ultimately implemented. The essential components norming guide also helps teams identify, clarify, and norm around those things that will be essential for successful implementation.

This tool helps leaders get clear on the *what* and the *how* before building the *who* and the *when*. Research on MTSS frameworks highlights the importance of clearly defined core components. Without this clarity, implementation becomes inconsistent and fragmented across schools. Schools that explicitly define essential components are better able to maintain fidelity while still allowing for local adaptation.

Here are common essential components I have seen school districts and states include in their MTSS frameworks:

- Leadership
- Data use
- Tiered supports
- Communication and collaboration
- Building Capacity
- Equity and access

Readiness Reflection: Have we named what it is that we're actually building, or are we guessing as we go?

4. Self-Assessment Instrument

Once the foundational elements, aka essential components, are defined, it's time to look inward. The self-assessment helps MTSS teams assess their current reality: *What's working? Where are we just checking boxes?*

Once MTSS is in place and implementation has begun, schools must continuously reflect on implementation progress. The self-assessment is the internal reflection tool used by school teams to evaluate the strength and fidelity of their current practices. Research on continuous improvement models within MTSS emphasizes the importance of ongoing self-assessment and data-driven reflection. Schools that regularly evaluate their implementation are more likely to identify barriers early and adjust practices before problems become systemic.

This tool also helps schools and districts identify needed supports. The self-assessment is a tool that is aligned to your essential components and includes a rating system based on the implementation science model to give schools a gauge of where they are in the MTSS implementation process.

Readiness Reflection: Where are our strengths giving us momentum, and where do we need to dig deeper before scaling?

5. MTSS Action Planning Template

After assessing your readiness, needs, and gaps, it's time to act. The MTSS action plan template turns self-assessment insights into concrete next steps. This template helps schools and districts prioritize goals for implementation, assign responsibilities, set deadlines, and establish a follow-up and accountability process.

Research on implementation planning confirms that structured action planning significantly increases implementation success by translating strategy into measurable actions (Metz & Bartley, 2012). Schools that move directly from assessment to action planning create clear pathways for improvement rather than relying on informal or inconsistent follow-through.

<u>Bonus Tip</u>: Schools can use this template to align their MTSS work with their school improvement plans. When MTSS is embedded into your larger strategy, it becomes more sustainable.

Readiness Reflection: Are we planning with accountability or hoping things fall into place?

The bottom line is this: tools support fidelity and sustainability. Implementation science emphasizes that structured tools such as readiness assessments, fidelity rubrics, and action planning templates play a critical role in sustaining educational initiatives.

Research examining schoolwide implementation of multi-tiered frameworks found that schools that used structured self-assessment and planning tools demonstrated stronger implementation fidelity and greater long-term sustainability than schools relying primarily on informal processes.

We know that tools do not replace leadership. But they do translate leadership vision into consistent organizational practice. MTSS tools don't implement the work for you. But they do something just as powerful: they make the invisible visible. They expose the cracks. They clarify what matters. They build consistency. But most importantly, they help you lead from a place of readiness, not reaction. These tools aren't about making the work easier. They're about making your system stronger.

So ask yourself: Which of these will help me slow down, assess what's real, and build what's right for our students and our staff?

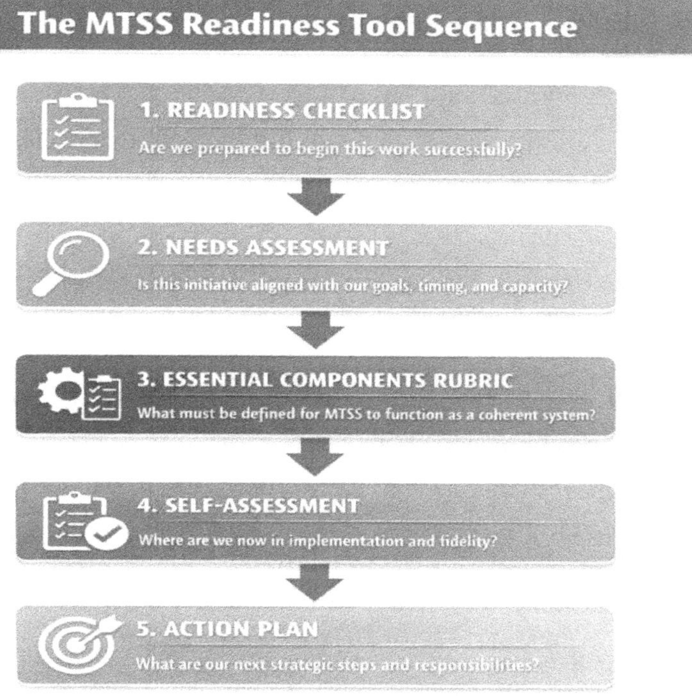

Figure 2:

This sequence illustrates how readiness tools function together as a system. Rather than jumping directly into implementation, schools move through a structured process that clarifies readiness, defines expectations, assesses current reality, and establishes a clear path forward.

Accessing the MTSS Readiness Toolkit

The tools introduced in this chapter are designed to support leaders in doing readiness work with clarity and intention. To ensure these tools remain practical, usable, and adaptable to real school and district contexts, a curated set of the signature tools referenced in this chapter is available to readers of this book through the MTSS Readiness Toolkit

— a guided implementation series designed to support leaders as they apply this work in their own systems.

The toolkit is released as a sequenced experience. The first tool is sent immediately upon signup, with additional tools and accompanying guidance delivered over the weeks that follow. This cadence is intentional: it mirrors the way effective leaders actually adopt new practices –one focused move at a time, with space to apply, reflect, and refine before the next.

These tools are intended to be used as leadership instruments, not compliance documents. They are most effective when applied thoughtfully, revisited over time, and used to surface honest conversations about system readiness, capacity, and alignment.

To join the Readiness Toolkit community and begin the series, visit: https://lp.constantcontactpages.com/sl/bwhyga4/ReadinessToolkit

While these tools can support meaningful planning and reflection, they do not replace leadership judgment, collaboration, or sustained system work. Readiness cannot be downloaded. It must be built. These tools exist to help you do that work with greater clarity and confidence.

A Note About What Comes Next

While this book focuses on getting your system ready, and this chapter explains the tools to do that, it's important to know that MTSS implementation doesn't stop here. Once you're ready and your foundation is in place, you'll need other tools to support MTSS implementation, in addition to those mentioned in this chapter. Tools such as intervention tracking, progress monitoring, fidelity checks, or even a district MTSS handbook or guidebook. These tools, while important, belong in the next phase of the work, and rushing to use them before your system is ready can lead to misalignment, confusion, and implementation fatigue. So for now, stay grounded in readiness, and those tools will be waiting for you…in my next book!

CHAPTER 6

The Stages of Implementation for MTSS

MTSS implementation is not just a strategy; it's a science (Fixsen et al., 2005; Metz & Bartley, 2012). Built on the principles of implementation science, MTSS provides schools with a research-backed, evidence-based framework that works . The stages of implementation serve as a guide, outlining what key activities should occur at each step and helping schools navigate the complexities of scaling MTSS practices for sustainability. In this chapter, we will explore the four stages of implementation and discuss how they relate to readiness and building and sustaining a strong MTSS framework.

Implementation science is the foundation of MTSS success. It provides a systematic approach for building foundational systems, scaling practices, and ensuring sustainability. The stages of implementation are tried and true, giving schools a roadmap to follow as they adopt MTSS. These stages help educators anticipate challenges, identify key activities, and maintain focus on the long-term goal of embedding MTSS as part of the "way we do school".

Implementation as a Test of System Readiness

There is a natural assumption that once a system has engaged in readiness work, implementation should follow with clarity and momentum. Leaders expect that the structures they have designed will begin to function, that teams will execute with consistency, and that the work will begin to produce visible outcomes. On the surface, that expectation makes sense. After all, preparation is meant to position a system for action, right?

But what often goes unexamined is what implementation actually requires of a system once that action begins.

Implementation is not simply the next step after readiness. It is the point at which the system is asked to perform under the conditions it has created. It is where planning gives way to practice, where expectations move beyond conversation, and where the system must demonstrate whether it can operate with the level of consistency, alignment, and clarity that the work demands.

This is where the connection between readiness and implementation becomes critical.

Implementation science has long established that complex change does not occur all at once. It unfolds over time, moving through identifiable stages that reflect the system's progression from initial exploration to sustained practice. These stages are not simply markers of progress; they represent shifts in what the system is capable of doing consistently.

What is often misunderstood, however, is how directly those stages are shaped by the work that preceded them.

Readiness is not left behind when implementation begins. It carries forward into every stage. The degree to which a system has established alignment, built capacity, clarified expectations, and strengthened its structures determines how implementation will unfold. In that sense, implementation does not introduce new challenges as much as it reveals the extent to which the system is prepared to manage the ones that already exist.

When readiness has been developed with intention, implementation tends to feel disciplined, even when it is demanding. The system is able to absorb the work because the foundational conditions are strong enough to support it. Teams understand their roles. Decision-making processes are clear. Data is used with purpose. Variability exists, but it is limited and addressable. The system may not be perfect, but it is stable enough to improve. If readiness has been incomplete or parts of it are skipped, implementation will look completely different.

What appears to be forward movement is often accompanied by an undercurrent of inconsistency. Teams are meeting, but outcomes are uneven. Practices are in place, but they are not applied consistently across classrooms or buildings. Data is collected, but its use varies depending on who is interpreting it. Leaders find themselves navigating competing priorities while attempting to maintain direction. The work is happening, but it is not yet functioning as a system, and this is where many systems begin to misread their own progress.

Implementation creates visibility. Structures that once existed only in planning documents and binders are now observable in practice. Because of that visibility, there has been a tendency to equate activity with effectiveness. If teams are meeting, if interventions are scheduled, and data are being reviewed, it can appear that the system is moving forward as intended.

But here's what we have to remember: visibility is not the same as consistency, and activity is not the same as alignment.

The stages of implementation are not defined by what has been put in place. They are defined by how reliably the system can carry out the work across contexts and over time. Each stage places a different demand on the system, and those demands cannot be met through effort alone. They require the system to function in ways that cannot be improvised in the moment.

This is why implementation cannot be understood apart from readiness. Implementation does not confirm readiness; it tests it under pressure.

The work does not begin when implementation starts. It just makes the work more observable. And what becomes observable is not just the work itself, but the condition of the system attempting to carry it out.

In the sections that follow, we will examine the stages of implementation more closely, not as a sequence to move through as quickly as possible, but as a progression that requires disciplined leadership at each point. The goal is not simply to identify where a system is within the stages, but to understand what each stage is asking of the system and how leaders can respond in ways that strengthen, rather than strain, the work.

The difference between systems that sustain implementation and those that struggle is not whether they reach implementation.

It is whether they understand what implementation is actually revealing.

What Leaders Must Understand Before Moving Through the Stages

Before examining the stages of implementation, let's clarify how they should be understood.

Many systems treat the stages as steps to move through as quickly as possible, rather than as indicators of what the system can execute with consistency. The stages are not a timeline; they are measures of capacity. Each stage reflects not what has been put in place, but what the system can carry out reliably over time.

A system can introduce structures that align with one stage and still be operating in another. Teams may be meeting, interventions may be scheduled, and data may be collected, but if those practices are not carried out consistently across contexts, the system is not really progressing in that stage.

The mere presence of activity creates the illusion of movement. Leaders see the work happening and assume that the system is advancing through the stages. But what is often advancing is not the system's ability to perform consistently; it is the system's ability to produce visible action.

This means that movement from one stage to the next is not something that can be forced through urgency or effort. Effective movement through the stages occurs when the system has developed enough alignment, clarity, and capacity to operate predictably without relying on individual effort to hold the work together.

When that condition is present, the system stabilizes. When that condition is not present, the system experiences strain, and leaders find themselves addressing the same issues over and over again. Teams require constant clarification. And practices continue to vary across contexts. The work seems to continue, but it never stabilizes.

As a final thought, progress through the stages is not proven by activity, but by the system's ability to sustain the work consistently and reliably.

Let's take a look at the four stages of implementation and some of the key activities that take place during each stage.

The Four Stages of Implementation (Fixsen et al., 2005, 2019)

Stage 1. Exploration

The exploration stage is all about preparation. This is where the bulk of readiness work is either taken seriously or bypassed completely. The exploration stage is often misunderstood as the beginning of implementation, when in reality, it is the system's first opportunity to determine whether now is the right time for implementation, and under what conditions.

During exploration, schools and districts examine their current state, assess needs, and engage stakeholders to build understanding around the work. On the surface, these activities appear straightforward. But the strength of this stage is not in the completion of tasks. It is in the quality of the decisions that come from them.

A system that is engaging in exploration with discipline is not asking, "Is MTSS a good idea?" We know that has already been established. The question being answered here is whether the system, as it currently operates, is positioned to take on the work without creating fragmentation.

This requires a level of honesty that systems do not always sustain in practice.

Competing priorities must be acknowledged, not minimized. Capacity must be evaluated beyond staffing. Existing systems must be examined for stability, not just presence. And most importantly, leaders must be willing to determine not just what needs to be added, but what may need to shift or stop in order for the work to be sustained.

If exploration is approached as just a confirmation process, then the system moves forward because it feels expected to do so. Not because it is prepared.

On the other hand, when exploration is approached as a readiness condition, the outcome is much different. The system gains clarity around what it can realistically carry, clarity around where alignment is lacking, and clarity around what conditions need to be strengthened before implementation begins.

Now that the system has agreed on clarified conditions, here is also where many systems make their first critical mistake. They mistake agreement for readiness.

Just because stakeholders are engaged, conversations are taking place, and there's general support for moving forward, this does not mean the system is aligned in practice and ready to move forward. Agreement does not ensure consistency. And consistency is what implementation will ultimately demand.

A system does not move into the next stage just because exploration has been discussed. It moves forward when the system has developed enough clarity and alignment to realistically support what comes next. Exploration lays the groundwork for change by ensuring that schools start with a clear understanding of why MTSS is needed and what it will take to succeed.

Key activities that systems could be doing in this stage:

- Assessing district and/or school needs and priorities through needs assessments.
- Engaging stakeholders, including educators, families, and community members, to build awareness and gather input.
- Researching MTSS and its benefits to build a case for implementation.
- Examining current systems for alignment, stability, and capacity
- Determining readiness and identifying potential barriers that impact implementation if left unaddressed.

Leadership Signal to Watch

If the system is moving forward because the work is expected rather than because the system is prepared, a readiness gap has already been established.

Stage 2. Installation

Installation is where the planning gets concrete, and this stage is also a crucial part of readiness. This stage involves developing the systems, practices, and logistics needed to bring MTSS to life. Think of this stage as creating the blueprint for success.

Installation is where many systems begin to feel ready, because the work becomes visible. Teams are formed, roles are defined, professional learning is planned, and systems for data and intervention are established. So, on the surface, it looks like the system is preparing well.

But installation is not about simply building the structures. It is about determining whether those structures will function as intended.

This is where readiness shifts from planning to operational clarity. It requires more than identifying who will do the work; it requires ensuring that expectations are understood, decision-making processes are defined, and systems are aligned in a way that supports consistent execution. Without that level of clarity, even well-designed structures will stall.

The presence of teams, protocols, and plans can create the impression that the system is prepared to move forward. But if roles are unclear, if expectations vary, or if data systems are not yet guiding decisions consistently, the system is not ready for implementation. It is prepared in design but not yet in function.

Installation is not complete when the system is built. It is complete when the system is clear enough to be used consistently and can function reliably.

Key activities that systems could be doing in this stage:

- Establishing district and school-level MTSS teams.
- Defining roles and responsibilities with clearly defined roles and decision-making.
- Developing professional learning that builds practical, not just conceptual, capacity.
- Conducting readiness assessments to ensure all pieces are in place.
- Establishing expectations for data systems and intervention protocols.
- Aligning systems, structures, and resources to support consistent implementation.

Leadership Signal to Watch

If the system looks organized but requires constant clarification to function, readiness has not yet been established.

Stage 3. Initial Implementation

Initial implementation is where the work becomes real.

Practices are finally put into motion, and the system begins to operate under the expectations that have been established. This is often described as the "messy middle," not because the work is failing, but because the system is now being tested in real conditions.

In systems where readiness has been built with discipline, this stage is demanding but still very manageable. Practices may still vary, but the system has enough alignment to identify inconsistencies and address them with intention. Feedback loops begin to strengthen the work rather than disrupt it.

In systems where readiness has been incomplete, strain becomes more visible. Teams require ongoing clarification. Practices vary widely. Leaders find themselves responding to issues rather than guiding the work forward. The system is active, but it is not yet stable.

This is where many systems experience inconsistency and assume something is wrong with the framework or the implementation itself. In reality, what they are seeing is the system's current capacity being revealed.

Initial Implementation is a very critical stage, as it is about the work. This stage can sometimes be the deciding factor as to whether MTSS will thrive or not. If schools fall short during this stage, it's usually because of these two things:

- **Underestimating the Effort:** Schools may not anticipate the time, energy, and commitment required for successful implementation.
- **Expecting Quick Results:** MTSS is a marathon, not a sprint. Unrealistic expectations can lead to frustration and burnout.

It's important to realize that initial implementation of MTSS or any new initiative can span anywhere from 9–24 months (Fixsen et al., 2005), and success at this stage requires patience, persistence, and a commitment to continuous improvement.

Key activities that systems could be doing in this stage:

- Piloting MTSS in selected schools or grade levels.
- Monitoring progress and collecting data to evaluate effectiveness.
- Providing ongoing coaching and support to staff as they adjust to new practices.
- Identifying and addressing inconsistencies before expanding the work.
- Addressing resistance and problem-solving challenges as they arise.

Leadership Signal to Watch

If the system is expanding the work while practices remain inconsistent, it is moving beyond its current capacity.

Stage 4: Full Implementation

When schools make it to this point, they've usually had many months, or even years of trial and error. However, once they reach the full implementation stage, MTSS has become embedded into the district or school's operations. It is no longer seen as an initiative but as "the way we do school." Policies, practices, and systems are aligned, and continuous improvement ensures sustainability.

Full implementation is often misunderstood as the point where the work is complete, when in reality, it more reflects the point where the system no longer relies on effort to sustain the work.

At this stage, practices are now embedded into daily operations. Expectations are clear and consistently applied. Decision-making is guided by shared processes rather than individual interpretation. The system functions with a level of predictability that allows the work to continue, even as people and conditions change.

This stage is the result of readiness and disciplined implementation working together.

In systems that reach this stage, the work has moved beyond individuals. It is supported by structures, reinforced through leadership, and sustained through consistent practice. Improvement continues, but it is built on stability rather than constant correction. In other words, the foundation is now solid enough that growth can build naturally. Instead of reacting and correcting all the time, practices are stable, understood, and repeatable, and improvement comes from refining and deepening, not from starting over or patching problems.

In systems that have moved forward without adequate readiness work, this stage is difficult to reach. The work may continue, but variability will persist beneath the surface. Full implementation is not defined by how long the system has been engaged in the work. It is defined by how well the system can sustain it.

Key activities that systems could be doing in this stage:

- Embedding MTSS practices into district policies and daily operations.
- Maintaining ongoing professional development to continue building staff capacity.
- Using data to refine and improve practices, not just to monitor.
- Fostering a culture of continuous improvement to adapt to changes over time.
- Reinforcing stakeholder commitment and accountability across the system.

Sustainability is the ultimate goal of full implementation, and it is supported by the foundational work done in earlier stages. This stage ensures that MTSS is not just implemented but thrives over the long term.

Leadership Signal to Watch

If the work depends on specific individuals to maintain consistency, the system has not yet reached full implementation.

Why the Stages Matter

The stages of implementation provide more than just a roadmap; they offer a way to think strategically about readiness and the overall change process needed to implement MTSS successfully. Each stage builds on the one before it, ensuring that schools lay a solid foundation before scaling up practices. By following the stages, schools can avoid common pitfalls, anticipate challenges, and create a culture of continuous improvement.

Implementation is not about perfection; it's about progress. By embracing the stages of implementation, schools can build MTSS frameworks that are not only evidence-based but also sustainable. Each stage is an opportunity to reflect, refine, and grow, ensuring that MTSS becomes the cornerstone of a culture that supports every student, every day.

CHAPTER 7

Common Readiness Pitfalls and How to Avoid Them

MTSS is powerful, but only when implemented with intention, clarity, and commitment. Unfortunately, many schools and districts dive in too quickly or overlook readiness, which leads to frustration, inconsistency, and eventually abandonment of the framework altogether. In this chapter, we'll shine a light on the most common pitfalls schools face when implementing MTSS and, more importantly, how to avoid them. Consider this your "watch out for this" guide as you move from planning to practice.

Pitfall #1: Rushing into Implementation Without Readiness

Let's name the real issue: most MTSS implementation failures happen because schools move too fast. Rushing into MTSS without readiness is not a minor misstep. It is the fastest way to guarantee confusion, staff resistance, and initiative fatigue. When leaders skip foundational work,

MTSS becomes another short-lived reform instead of a sustainable system. Readiness is not optional. It *is* the work. And when it's ignored, the consequences show up quickly and loudly.

When schools rush MTSS, the warning signs are predictable. Staff attend MTSS trainings without understanding how the pieces connect, leaving them confused about expectations and skeptical of the purpose. Practices vary widely from classroom to classroom because no shared system was established first. School leaders find themselves managing meetings, data, and interventions reactively, responding to problems instead of leading a coherent strategy. Over time, staff stop seeing MTSS as support and start seeing it as noise. And once that trust is lost, it is hard to rebuild.

Here's How to Avoid This Pitfall:

Use a readiness checklist and conduct a needs assessment **before** starting MTSS. Clearly communicate the why behind MTSS to all staff. Build your foundational elements first: MTSS teams and essential components. If this pitfall is showing up in your system, it's a readiness red flag. Pause, reflect, and go back to the foundation.

Pitfall #2: Treating MTSS as a Compliance Initiative

When MTSS is reduced to a checklist or audit requirement, it loses its impact almost immediately. What was designed to be a proactive system for supporting students becomes another task staff endure rather than a framework they believe in. In schools where MTSS is treated as compliance, it shows up only during walkthroughs, audits, or reporting cycles. Meetings focus on documentation instead of problem-solving. Staff see MTSS as "something administrators want," not as something that improves daily instructional practices and student outcomes. This is not a staff problem; it is a leadership framing problem.

Leaders set the tone for whether MTSS lives in binders or in classrooms. When MTSS is positioned as a requirement rather than a system for improving outcomes, buy-in erodes quickly. Over time, teams disengage, fidelity drops, and MTSS becomes the very thing it was never meant to be: another initiative that didn't last. When MTSS becomes "another thing to check off," it loses its power. True MTSS work is culture work. It must be woven into the way your school functions daily. And if you approach it with a deficit mindset, this is your sign: your system isn't ready yet.

Here's How to Avoid This Pitfall:

Frame MTSS as the way you do school, not as an extra program. MTSS should be interwoven into the fabric of the school and the district. Integrate MTSS language, goals, and practices into existing structures such as PLCs, walkthroughs, and school improvement plans. Empower all staff, not just intervention teams, to take ownership of MTSS. Model MTSS decision-making at the leadership level so staff see it in action, not just in documents.

Pitfall #3: Failing to Define Roles and Responsibilities

When roles are unclear, MTSS breaks down quickly. Teams stall, decisions are delayed, and accountability becomes diffuse. Without clarity, even motivated staff struggle to implement MTSS with fidelity. In schools where this pitfall exists, teachers are unsure who leads Tier 2 or Tier 3 interventions. Counselors, interventionists, and administrators assume someone else is responsible. Building leaders attend MTSS meetings sporadically or delegate the work entirely, unintentionally signaling that MTSS is optional.

MTSS requires intentional role definition and shared understanding. When leaders fail to clarify who owns which decisions, systems default to confusion. Clear roles create efficiency, consistency, and trust across the system. If your team is spinning in circles, check your readiness around role clarity.

Here's How to Avoid This Pitfall:

Develop a clear MTSS role matrix that defines responsibilities at each tier.
Train teams together so roles are understood in context, not isolation.
Ensure building leaders are active participants in MTSS decision-making.
Make MTSS a standing topic in leadership meetings and Professional Learning Community (PLC) meetings.

Pitfall #4: Ignoring Data or Using It Poorly

MTSS is built on data, yet many schools struggle to use it effectively. Data overload, inconsistent systems, and lack of training often lead teams to make decisions based on assumptions rather than evidence. When this pitfall is present, teams collect large amounts of data but lack clarity on what to analyze, how to interpret it, or how to respond. Meetings become reports instead of problem-solving sessions. Staff comply with data collection but disengage from its purpose.

Data should inform instructional moves and decisions. When it doesn't, MTSS becomes performative rather than purposeful. If your school is collecting data but not using it to drive instruction, it's time to assess your readiness around data fluency and system alignment.

Here's How to Avoid This Pitfall:

Provide ongoing training focused on data interpretation and instructional response. Use structured data protocols to guide MTSS meetings and PLCs. Align data collection directly to intervention decisions and progress monitoring. Provide regular professional learning on data analysis, differentiation, assessments, and decision-making. Keep your data dashboard simple, visual, and aligned to your essential components.

Pitfall #5: Leaving Leadership Out of the Process

MTSS implementation flounders if leaders are disconnected. Leaders must not only support MTSS—they must model it. MTSS cannot be delegated and sustained. When leaders distance themselves from the work, implementation weakens and accountability fades.. In schools experiencing this pitfall, MTSS is managed by a single coordinator, interventionist, or coach with limited authority. Leadership meetings rarely address MTSS outcomes. Strategic plans reference MTSS without clear expectations or metrics. This sends a clear message that MTSS is not a leadership priority. MTSS requires visible, consistent leadership involvement. When leaders are absent, the system lacks direction and momentum. When leaders are present, MTSS gains legitimacy and coherence.

Here's How to Avoid This Pitfall:

Make MTSS a standing agenda item in leadership meetings. Include MTSS metrics in school and district goals. Align MTSS goals with school and district priorities. Walk the talk. Leaders should attend MTSS professional learning sessions and model data-informed leadership. If this is a struggle in your building or district, don't ignore it…readiness starts at the top.

Pitfall #6: Overlooking Tier 1

Schools sometimes get so focused on Tiers 2 and 3 that they forget the foundation—Tier 1. Without strong universal instruction, your triangle will crumble. Strong Tier 1 instruction is the foundation of MTSS. When Tier 1 is weak, intervention systems become overloaded and unsustainable. Instructional quality varies widely across classrooms, and teams spend more time intervening than improving core instruction.

In schools where this pitfall exists, large numbers of students are referred to Tier 2 or Tier 3, and few supports or extensions exist for students who don't need intervention. I know you've heard this before, but it bears repeating here: You cannot intervene your way out of weak Tier 1. Leaders must prioritize universal instruction, consistency, and fidelity. Without this focus, MTSS becomes reactive rather than proactive and preventative. If Tier 1 is shaky, you're not ready for full MTSS implementation–you're still laying the foundation.

Here's How to Avoid This Pitfall:

Invest in Tier 1 first: evidence-based curriculum, instructional best practices, universal SEL and behavior supports. Build teacher capacity in establishing good instructional routines, scaffolding, differentiation, formative assessments, progress monitoring, classroom management, etc. Monitor Tier 1 fidelity with walkthroughs and classroom data and provide feedback to teachers on how to make instructional shifts based on these data.

Pitfall #7: Neglecting Adult Behavior Change

Remember: MTSS is just as much about changing adult practices as it is about supporting students. MTSS is not just a student support framework; it is a leadership and adult practice framework. When adult behavior remains unchanged, outcomes remain unchanged. This pitfall appears when staff continue using ineffective practices, resist feedback, or treat professional development as optional. Intervention protocols exist but are inconsistently followed. MTSS exposes adult practice, and like it or not, avoiding that reality undermines the entire system. Leaders must create conditions where reflection, coaching, and accountability are expected and supported. Adult learning is not secondary; it is central to MTSS success. If adults aren't changing, your system isn't ready to support students.

Here's How to Avoid This Pitfall:

Focus professional learning on reflection, coaching, and practical application. Use adult learning principles to design MTSS training. Celebrate early adopters and highlight the success stories.

Final thought

As we wrap up this chapter, know this: Pitfalls don't mean failure; they're just signals. What matters is how you respond to them. By proactively addressing these challenges and planning for them from the start, you can turn obstacles into learning opportunities.

MTSS is a journey. Expect bumps. But with the right mindset and a solid plan, you'll be ready to overcome them and stay the course toward meaningful, sustained impact. MTSS is not about perfection. It is about leadership commitment to doing the work well, even when it is uncomfortable. Readiness is your anchor and your starting line to avoiding these common pitfalls.

CONCLUSION

Lead with Readiness. Transform with Purpose.

Here is what no one tells you about readiness.

It will feel like you're slowing down when everyone else is moving. It will feel like caution when the culture is demanding speed. It will feel, at times, like you are the only person in the room who believes that the foundation matters more than the launch date. And in some rooms, you will be.

We operate in systems that have been designed to reward urgency. Move fast. Show progress. Launch the initiative. Demonstrate momentum. The pressure is real, and it does not come from bad intentions. It comes from a system that has confused activity with impact for so long that it no longer knows the difference.

Readiness pushes against that.

Readiness is a decision to say that the work will be done right before it is done quickly, that the foundation will be built before the structure goes up, that the system will be prepared to carry the work before it is asked to perform it.

That is why choosing readiness is the most purposeful decision a leader can make.

Not because it introduces something radical. But because it insists on something that systems have been conditioned to skip. And when leaders choose it anyway, they are doing something far harder than launching an initiative.

They are leading.

And while this book explored readiness through the lens of MTSS, that leadership extends far beyond a single framework. Literacy reforms, curriculum adoptions, intervention systems, and instructional coaching models all depend on the same underlying conditions. But when those conditions are absent, implementation struggles. When they are present, systems gain the stability required for meaningful change. MTSS simply gives us one of the clearest illustrations of what that readiness work actually requires.

Here is what that leadership makes possible. Eighteen months from now, in a system that chose readiness, the work does not depend on one coordinator holding it together. The practices do not disappear when a key leader transitions out. The data meetings are not performative. Teachers are not confused about what MTSS requires of them. They know. And because they know, they can do it consistently. And because they do it consistently, students receive the same quality of support regardless of which classroom they are in, which school they attend, or which teacher they have.

That is equity made operational.

In a system that skipped readiness, the same eighteen months looks different. The structures are there, but they require constant correction. Clarity has to be rebuilt every time a new person joins the team. The work is happening, but it is not sticking. And leaders are spending their energy on repair rather than on refinement.

The difference between those two systems is not effort; both worked hard. It is not intention; both wanted to get it right. The difference is the sequence. One system built the foundation first. The other is still trying to build it while the structure is already in motion.

There will be setbacks. There will be resistance. There will be moments when it feels like everything is moving too slowly, or like the work is not producing results fast enough to satisfy the people watching. That is part of this work. It does not mean the work is failing. It means the work is real.

You are reading this book because you understand that distinction. Or because you are beginning to. Either way, you are asking the right question: Is your system ready to do it in a way that will last?

That question is not always welcomed. It requires honesty that systems do not always reward. It requires leaders to name what is not working before they can build what will. You can have the best programs, the clearest data, and the strongest intentions, but without a foundation of readiness, none of it will last. Readiness is what separates initiatives that come and go from systems that stand the test of time.

But here is what I know after years of doing this work inside schools and districts that were trying, struggling, and sometimes succeeding: the leaders who changed outcomes were not the ones who moved the fastest. They were the ones who built systems intentionally and deliberately. They were the ones who asked the harder questions. They were the ones who chose readiness when no one else did.

Let this book be your launchpad, your blueprint, and your reminder that readiness is not about having all the answers. It is about asking the right questions and being bold enough to act on what you discover.

Readiness is the work.

And when you choose it fully, honestly, and unapologetically, you are not just preparing to implement a framework.

You are refusing to let another generation of students wait.

That is what readiness makes possible. Not just better systems, but better outcomes for every student, every educator, and every leader willing to do the work.

APPENDIX A

Readiness in Practice — Dilemmas for Leaders

By this point in the book, you have examined what readiness requires, how it is built, and how it reveals itself — or not — during implementation. You have seen how systems can appear to be functioning while still lacking the internal conditions needed to sustain the work. You have seen how activity masks as progress when the system has not yet stabilized, and how leaders can find themselves managing the appearance of implementation rather than the reality of it.

Understanding readiness conceptually, however, is not the same as leading through it under pressure.

Readiness is not assessed in a controlled moment of reflection. It is tested in the middle of decision-making -when timelines are compressed, expectations are high, and the system is already in motion. Leaders are rarely afforded the conditions to pause and evaluate with precision. Instead, they are required to make judgment calls while navigating competing priorities, incomplete information, and the very real pressure to show forward movement.

This is where many systems arrive at a crossroads. Not because leaders lack knowledge, but because the decisions that are most consequential to readiness are rarely framed that way. They are framed as implementation decisions. Compliance decisions. Operational decisions. When readiness is not explicitly named in those moments, systems move forward without the conditions that would allow the work to hold, and the cost of that is paid later, often quietly, and always at the expense of students.

That is why this appendix exists.

The dilemmas that follow are not hypothetical. They reflect the real situations leaders encounter when implementing MTSS inside systems that are complex, under-resourced, and expected to perform regardless. These are moments where the right next step is not self-evident, where urgency and readiness pull in different directions, and where the decision you're facing is not simply about what to do next, but about whether the system is genuinely prepared to do it well and sustain it over time.

Each dilemma is designed to surface tension, challenge assumptions, and sharpen your thinking and judgment, which cannot always be taught through frameworks alone. Read each dilemma not to confirm your thinking, but to test it.

1. Mandate vs. Readiness

When implementation is required, but the system doesn't have the alignment and capacity to sustain the work, what should take priority –meeting the mandate quickly or building the conditions that will allow the work to hold?

We know that mandates are not going to disappear. But neither will the damage caused by implementing something a system is not equipped to handle. Speed without readiness is just performance, not commitment. Leaders who prioritize checking the implementation box over building the internal conditions that make the work hold are not serving the mandate; they are protecting themselves from the discomfort of honest assessment. The more urgent question is this: what good is meeting a timeline if the work collapses twelve months later? True accountability requires leaders to move toward the mandate and name what is missing, advocate for what is needed, and structure the work in a sequence that the system can actually carry. It's really not a choice between the mandate and readiness. It's about whether you choose to be honest about both.

2. Activity vs. Progress

When teams are meeting, data is being reviewed, and structures are in place, but outcomes remain inconsistent, how do leaders determine whether the system is progressing or simply producing visible activity?

Meetings are not evidence of movement. Data reviews are not evidence of change. Structures are not evidence of function. The question is not are we doing the work; but rather, is the work changing anything. Leaders must be willing to audit what their activity is actually producing. If the same conversations are happening in October that happened in February, the system is not progressing — it is cycling. Progress has a direction. It moves students closer to something measurable. If the only thing a leader can point to is that the team met, the agenda was followed, and the data was shown, that is not progress. That is process. The two are not the same, and mistaking one for the other is how systems stay busy for years while outcomes remain unchanged.

3. System-Wide vs. Variable Readiness

When some schools or teams are operating with clarity and consistency while others are not, should implementation move forward across the system, or should leaders pace the work to protect coherence?

Pacing is not the problem here. Inconsistency is. When a system moves forward at a uniform pace regardless of variable readiness, what it creates is not consistency; it creates a wider gap between schools that can sustain the work and schools that are drowning in it quietly. Leaders must resist the idea that treating all schools the same is somehow fair. It is not. Different schools have different needs. Schools operating without clarity need differentiated support, not identical timelines. What protects coherence across a system is not uniform implementation speed; it is shared expectations, clear non-negotiables, and honest assessment of where each school actually is. Move forward where there is readiness. Stabilize where there is not. And never confuse motion across all schools with alignment across all schools.

4. Tier 1 vs. Intervention Pressure

When Tier 1 instruction is inconsistent, but there is pressure to expand intervention supports, what risk does the system create by addressing symptoms instead of stabilizing the foundation?

The risk is a system that mistakes busyness for growth. Expanding interventions on top of an unstable Tier 1 is the educational equivalent of building additional floors on a cracked foundation. The structure looks taller, but it is more fragile. When core instruction is inconsistent, intervention cannot compensate at scale. What it produces instead is a growing referral pipeline, overwhelmed interventionists, and students who cycle through supports without sustained improvement, because the place where they spend the majority of their instructional time, tier 1, is not yet reliable. Every resource invested in expanding intervention before stabilizing Tier 1 is a resource that will need to be reinvested later, often at greater cost. The pressure to add is real, but leaders must be willing to say out loud: we cannot intervene our way out of a Tier 1 problem.

5. Resistance vs. System Clarity

When staff resistance emerges, is it a reflection of unwillingness, or a signal that expectations, roles, and support have not been clearly defined within the system?

Resistance is information. Before a leader responds to it as a personnel problem, they must first interrogate the system that produced it. When staff do not know precisely what they are responsible for, what success looks like in their role, or where they are supposed to go when they are uncertain, resistance is a rational response. It is not defiance; it is a symptom of ambiguity. That said, clarity does not eliminate all resistance. Some resistance persists even after expectations are clear, roles are defined, and support is in place, and that is a different conversation. The discipline of leadership is in knowing which one you are dealing with. Ask first: have we been clear enough, specific enough, and supportive enough for this expectation to be reasonable? If the honest answer is no, the work begins there. If the answer is yes, then the leader must act on that truth.

6. Speed vs. Sustainability

When urgency is driving decisions, how do leaders determine whether the system is moving forward with intention or advancing beyond what it can sustain?

The signal is usually in what is being skipped. When systems are advancing beyond their capacity, the first casualties are depth of understanding, quality of feedback loops, and the time required for staff to internalize what they are being asked to do. Leaders under urgency often confuse launch with implementation and roll-out with embedding. A system is moving with intention when people inside it can explain not just what they are doing, but why the sequence was designed this way, what comes next, and what they are responsible for ensuring. When staff can only describe activity — not purpose, not sequence, not personal accountability — the system has likely moved past what it can hold. Urgency is not a strategy. It is a pressure point. Leaders are responsible for ensuring the pressure does not override the judgment that makes the work worth doing.

7. Data vs. Interpretation

When data is available but decisions vary across teams, is the issue the data itself, or the absence of shared expectations for how it should be used?

The data is rarely the problem. Not having a shared lens for reading it almost always is. When teams look at the same numbers and arrive at different conclusions, different thresholds for concern, different timelines for response, or different definitions of who is responsible, the system has a coherence problem, not a data problem. More data or more testing will not solve this. Better data will not solve this. What solves this is a clearly defined, explicitly taught, consistently reinforced framework for what the data means and what it requires. Leaders must stop treating data literacy as a skill to develop and start treating a unified lens for interpretation and analysis as the expectation to build. Teams that share data without sharing a decision-making framework are not operating a data system — they are hosting a weekly exercise in disagreement dressed up as collaboration.

8. Ownership vs. Participation

When multiple people are involved in the work, but follow-through is inconsistent, who is really responsible for ensuring that decisions are carried out across the system?

Shared responsibility without named accountability is how nothing gets done collectively while everyone is involved. Participation means you were in the room. Ownership means you are answerable for the outcome. These are not the same, and systems that treat them as interchangeable produce exactly the follow-through patterns described here: everyone attended, no one was responsible. Leaders must be explicit after every decision; name who owns it, what completion looks like, and when and how accountability will occur. If a leader cannot answer those questions about a decision their team made, the decision is not yet complete. Involvement distributes effort. Accountability concentrates responsibility. Involvement gets people to the table. Accountability determines what leaves the table and actually happens in the system. Both are necessary, but only one determines whether the work actually moves.

9. Consistency vs. Autonomy

When variability exists across classrooms or schools, where should leaders draw the line between professional autonomy and the need for consistent, system-wide expectations?

Autonomy is not the freedom to produce different outcomes for different children based on individual preference. That is the line. Professional autonomy is meaningful and worth protecting in the spaces where local judgment, relationship knowledge, and instructional responsiveness live. But it does not extend to the foundational structures that a system has determined are non-negotiable for all students —

universal screening, core instructional routines, data review protocols, tiered intervention processes. When variability in those areas produces variability in student access, the conversation is no longer about autonomy. It is about equity. Leaders who avoid this distinction in the name of staff morale or political safety are making a quiet choice about whose children get a consistent experience. That choice has consequences, and naming it directly is part of what leadership at this level requires.

10. Implementation vs. Capacity

When the system appears to be implementing, but requires constant correction and oversight to function, is the work truly being implemented, or is the system operating beyond its current capacity?

True implementation is present when the work continues with fidelity in the absence of direct oversight. If leaders must be in every room, correct every mistake, and re-explain every expectation repeatedly, what they are doing is creating symptoms of a system that has not yet internalized what it is doing or why. When a leader's physical presence is the variable that determines whether something happens correctly, the system is not functioning; the leader is functioning on the system's behalf. The work is being upheld by the person, not by the structure. This distinction matters enormously for scale and for sustainability. Leaders must ask: if I stepped back for sixty days, would my school hold, or fall apart? Whatever the honest answer is, that is the actual level of implementation. The rest is maintenance disguised as progress.

APPENDIX B

Frequently Asked Readiness Questions

This section is for the real questions. Questions that I've been asked throughout the course of my educational career. The ones that keep leaders up at night, the ones that come up in hallway conversations, and the ones that don't always have simple answers. These FAQs aren't just about MTSS. They're about change. Culture. Readiness. Leadership. And what it takes to move an entire school system forward when you're not sure everyone is ready. Let's take a look.

1. What if I'm the only one who believes in this work?

You're not alone. Many leaders start their MTSS journey with little to no buy-in. It's discouraging, but it's not the end. Start with those who are willing. Use the readiness tools to show—not tell—where gaps exist. And keep modeling what it looks like to lead with vision, even when others don't see it yet. Sometimes early adopters and small leadership coalitions can often drive system-wide transformation before broader buy-in develops.

2. How do I know if our school is truly ready to implement MTSS?

Start with a readiness checklist and needs assessment. Ask: Do we have a leadership team? Do we have time, space, and energy to do this well? MTSS is not a plug-and-play model. If you're not ready, that's a signal to slow down and build the foundation first. Implementation science emphasizes that organizational readiness (leadership alignment, infrastructure, and staff capacity) is one of the strongest predictors of successful implementation (Weiner, 2009).

3. What if teachers think MTSS is just more work?

That's valid, and they're not wrong. At first, it *will* feel like more. But when MTSS is done right, it eventually *replaces* ineffective work with focused, effective practices. The key is helping teachers see the long-term benefit and involving them in shaping the process, not just delivering it to them. Sustainable change requires teacher ownership and shared leadership, not top-down mandates.

4. Our Tier 1 isn't strong. Should we even be thinking about MTSS yet?

Yes, but not in the way you might think. MTSS isn't just about interventions. It's a framework that helps strengthen Tier 1. Use the first two stages of implementation to assess gaps that could be hindering Tier 1 instruction. Tier 1 is the foundation, and MTSS gives you the tools to build a strong foundation that leads to increased student outcomes.

5. What's the first thing I should actually *do* to get started?

Form your leadership team. Establish your vision. And assess your readiness. Don't rush into rollout. Start with clarity, then build systems. Planning *is* implementation, so don't skip it. Effective implementation research shows that strong leadership teams and structured planning processes significantly improve the likelihood of successful system change (Fixsen et al., 2005, 2019).

6. We've tried MTSS before and it didn't stick. What's different this time?

This time, you're prioritizing the readiness part of it...the preparation and planning part. You're not jumping in with tools and trainings; you're building systems, norms, and a culture of shared ownership. That's the difference. Start with reflection, not reaction. Studies examining MTSS implementation consistently find that systems built without sufficient preparation often struggle to sustain the work over time.

7. What if we don't have the time, people, or resources to do this right now?

That's a readiness issue, and it's okay. MTSS can't be built on burnout. Acknowledge the bandwidth reality, and focus on building momentum with what you *do* have. Sometimes starting small is the most strategic move. Implementation research emphasizes that sustainable change occurs when organizations build capacity gradually rather than attempting rapid system-wide adoption.

8. How do we make MTSS last beyond one leader or one school year?

Build it into your system's DNA. That means job descriptions, PD plans, school improvement plans, and onboarding processes. MTSS can't live in one person. It must live in your structures and culture. Sustainable school improvement requires institutionalization, embedding practices into systems rather than individuals.

9. How do we shift mindsets around data and accountability without creating fear?

Model transparency. Celebrate learning and improvement, not perfection. Normalize saying, "We're not there yet, but here's where we're going." Use data to inform, not to shame. Research on data-informed decision making highlights the importance of building a culture of trust so that educators view data as a tool for improvement rather than evaluation (Datnow & Hubbard, 2016).

10. Do we have to start with all three tiers at once?

Nope. In fact, many systems find success by strengthening Tier 1 practices first. Then layer on Tier 2 and Tier 3 with intentional planning. MTSS is scalable, and pacing it well supports sustainability. Strong Tier 1 systems significantly reduce the number of students requiring intensive interventions.

11. What if our district leadership isn't fully on board?

Then start where you can. District alignment is ideal, but school-level leadership can still move the work forward. Document your progress. Show impact. I have seen success at the school level become the model for district-wide adoption. It may seem backwards, but it can work.

12. How do I get families involved in our MTSS process?

Start by shifting how you communicate. Don't just send home data; share the *why* behind the supports. Invite families into planning conversations. Offer interpreter services, if needed. And ask them what they need, not just what you think they need. Meaningful family engagement strengthens student outcomes and improves school improvement efforts.

13. How do I create buy-in without overwhelming my staff?

Connect the dots. Show how MTSS simplifies (not complicates) what they already care about: helping students succeed. Start with listening. Co-create solutions. And celebrate progress early and often.

14. Can MTSS really work in a small or rural district?

Yes! But it may look different. Leverage cross-role teams. Share responsibilities creatively. Focus on systems, not size. MTSS isn't about volume. It's about alignment, clarity, and responsiveness to the needs.

15. How do we maintain MTSS through leadership transitions?

Document everything, and develop an MTSS playbook or framework guide. Cross-train staff. Embed MTSS in your district's onboarding process. Make the system leader-proof, not leader-dependent.

16. What if we're doing the work, but we're not sure we're doing it *right*?

You're not alone. That's where the self-assessment and fidelity tools come in handy. Ask for feedback from schools and districts that have seen success and are willing to share their process, struggles, and success with you. Give yourself permission to learn as you go. Remember: Progress, not perfection, is the goal.

17. We don't have any intervention programs. How do we build supports without a budget?

You don't need expensive boxed programs to start supporting students. Use what you already have--existing instructional time, small groups, and internal expertise. Focus on strengthening Tier 1 instruction and using small-group reteach blocks intentionally. You can also create simple intervention menus, peer tutoring, check-in/check-out systems, and high-leverage strategies like repeated reading or visual supports. MTSS isn't about buying a program. It's about using your resources strategically and consistently.

In conclusion

You don't need all the answers to get started. But you *do* need the courage to ask the right questions. Choose your starting point. Revisit this section as new challenges arise. And remember, readiness is not about having everything in place. It's about building the mindset and preparing your system to respond with purpose.

References

Datnow, A., & Hubbard, L. (2016). Teacher capacity for and beliefs about data-driven decision making: A literature review of international research. *Teachers College Record, 118*(11), 1–44.

Durlak, J. A., & DuPre, E. P. (2008). Implementation matters: A review of research on the influence of implementation on program outcomes. *American Journal of Community Psychology, 41*(3–4), 327–350. https://doi.org/10.1007/s10464-008-9165-0

Dymnicki, A., Wandersman, A., Osher, D., Grigorescu, V., & Huang, L. (2014). Willing, able, ready: Basics and policy implications of readiness as a key component for implementation of evidence-based interventions. *Translational Behavioral Medicine, 4*(3), 245–255.

Fixsen, D. L., Blase, K. A., Metz, A., & Van Dyke, M. (2019). Implementation science and practice: A decade of progress and future directions. *Journal of Behavioral Health Services & Research, 46*(2), 169–175.

Fixsen, D. L., Naoom, S. F., Blase, K. A., Friedman, R. M., & Wallace, F. (2005). *Implementation research: A synthesis of the literature.* University of South Florida, Louis de la Parte Florida Mental Health Institute, National Implementation Research Network.

Forman, S. G., Olin, S. S., Hoagwood, K. E., Crowe, M., & Saka, N. (2020). Evidence-based interventions in schools: Developers' views of implementation barriers and facilitators. *School Mental Health, 12*, 404–418.

Fullan, M. (2007). *The new meaning of educational change* (4th ed.). Teachers College Press.

Khalifa, M., Gooden, M. A., & Davis, J. E. (2016). Culturally responsive school leadership: A synthesis of the literature. *Review of Educational Research, 86*(4), 1272–1311.

McIntosh, K., & Goodman, S. (2016). *Integrated multi-tiered systems of support: Blending RTI and PBIS*. Guilford Press.

Metz, A., & Bartley, L. (2012). Active implementation frameworks for program success. *Zero to Three Journal, 32*(4), 11–18.

Metz, A., & Louison, L. (2019). *The Hexagon Tool: Exploring context for successful program implementation*. National Implementation Research Network.

National Center on Intensive Intervention. (2017). *Self-Assessment of MTSS (SAM)*. U.S. Department of Education, Office of Special Education Programs.

Scott, B.A., Stilwell, S.M., Pearson, Z.V. *et al.* Interventions to address racism in disciplinary actions in k-12 schools: A systematic review. *Prev Sci* (2025).

Skiba, R. J., Mediratta, K., & Rausch, M. K. (2016). Inequality in School Discipline : research and practice to reduce disparities. Palgrave Macmillan US.

Sugai, G., & Horner, R. (2020). School-wide positive behavioral interventions and supports: durability, fidelity, and equity. *Exceptional Children*, *86*(2), 120-136.

Sullivan, A. L., Nguyen, T., & Shaver, E. (2022). Foundations of equitycentered MTSS. Equity by Design. Midwest & Plains Equity Assistance Center (MAP EAC).

Weiner, B. J. (2009). A theory of organizational readiness for change. *Implementation Science, 4*(67), 1–9.

Stay Connected

with Dr. Carpia Naylor

Thank you for reading *The Readiness Gap*. My hope is that this book has challenged your thinking, sharpened your leadership lens, and helped you see readiness as a necessary condition for meaningful and sustainable implementation.

If this work resonated with you, I would love to stay connected.

Whether you are a school leader, district leader, educator, coach, or organization seeking support with MTSS readiness, literacy leadership, systems alignment, implementation planning, or professional learning, you are invited to reach out.

Website
carpianaylor.com

Email
hello@carpianaylor.com

LinkedIn
linkedin.com/in/dr-carpia-naylor

Substack
substack.com/@drcarpianaylor

For speaking, consulting, leadership support, professional learning, or collaboration inquiries, please visit my website or contact me directly by email.

Let's continue the work of building systems that are ready.

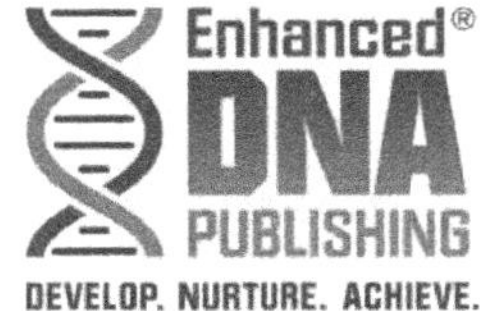
Enhanced®
DNA
PUBLISHING
DEVELOP. NURTURE. ACHIEVE.

www.ingramcontent.com/pod-product-compliance
Lightning Source LLC
LaVergne TN
LVHW010925110826
845149LV00013B/2488

9781967577132